ECONOMIC CHANGE IN PRECOLONIAL AFRICA

Supplementary Evidence

Philip D. Curtin

ECONOMIC CHANGE IN PRECOLONIAL AFRICA

Supplementary Evidence

The University of Wisconsin Press

Published 1975
The University of Wisconsin Press
Box 1379, Madison, Wisconsin 53701
The University of Wisconsin Press, Ltd.
70 Great Russell Street, London

First printing

Printed in the United States of America
For LC CIP information see the colophon

ISBN 0-299-06650-9

CONTENTS

TABLES

viii   List of Tables

NOTE

This supplement to *Economic Change in Precolonial Africa* has been separated from the main volume as a device for setting aside from the principal findings of that study the kind of information useful for further investigation. The main volume, for example, contains statistical and other data that are necessary to sustain its own argument, while this volume contains the raw data that went to make it up. In the same way, the footnotes to the main volume contain full citations at the first mention of each work, while this volume has the full bibliography systematically presented. Each volume contains its own index.

ABBREVIATIONS

AM	Archive de la Marine, Paris
ANF	Archives nationales de France, Paris
ANF-OM	Archives nationales de France, section Outre-Mer
ANS	Archives nationales du Sénégal
BIFAN	*Bulletin de l'Institut fondamental de l'Afrique noire;* formerly *Institut français de l'Afrique noire*
BN	Bibliothèque nationale, Paris
C6	In reference to ANF, carries the unstated implication that the indication is the colonial series of documents
CC	Curtin Collection of oral traditions of Bundu and Gajaaga, on deposit at IFAN, Dakar, and at the African Studies Association, Center for African Oral Data, Archive of Traditional Music, Maxwell Hall, Indiana University, Bloomington
CEA	*Cahiers d'études africaines*
CEHSAOF	*Bulletin du Comité des études historiques et scientifiques de l'Afrique occidentale française*
CI	Compagnie des Indes
CO	Colonial Office series, Public Record Office, London
DEA	Direction des affaires étrangères
FF, NA	Fonds français, nouvelles acquisitions, Bibliothèque nationale
IFAN	Institut fondamental de l'Afrique noire, Dakar
JAH	*Journal of African History*
JHSN	*Journal of the Historical Society of Nigeria*
JRGS	*Journal of the Royal Geographical Society*
MC	French Ministry of Colonies or Ministry of the Navy
PP	British Parliamentary Sessional Papers
PRO	Public Record Office, London
RAC	Royal African Company
RHCF	*Revue d'histoire des colonies françaises, Revue française d'histoire d'outre-mer*
RMM	*Revue du monde musulman*
Supplement	*Economic Change in Precolonial Africa: Supplementary Evidence*
T	Treasury series, Public Record Office, London

xi

APPENDICES

1 | PATTERNS OF CLIMATE AND DISEASE

The pattern of drought and disease is an important factor especially in the history of a place like Senegambia with its marginal rainfall and difficult disease environment. The chronicles of drought, famine, and disease that can be picked up, even from somewhat skimpy sources, help to support some of the generalizations in chapter 1; even more, they add to the mass of available data for studies in historical climatology. Studies in this field are only beginning in West Africa, but a comparison between the Senegambian data and those published by Sékéné Mody Cissoko for the Niger bend already helps show the outlines of an historical pattern over a long segment of desert-savanna fringe, as can be seen in· the following chronicles.

CHRONICLE OF DROUGHT AND FAMINE IN SENEGAMBIA, 1639-1853

1639-42 Famine in coastal Senegambia and Guinea-Bissau, so serious that it was remembered in 1681 as a worse famine than the one then in progress.[1]
1676 Drought in the lower valley of the Senegal.[2]
1681 Drought and food shortages in the vicinity of Saint Louis, and throughout the Wolof-speaking region.[3]
1685 Drought and food shortages near Saint Louis.[4]
1688-89 Very low rainfall in the region of Bambuhu and the upper Faleme, beginning with a bad rainy season in 1688, a second in 1689, but recovery of good rains in 1690.[5]
c. 1705-21 Prolonged low rainfall on the Cape Verde Islands, affecting all the archipelago to some extent, but forcing the complete depopulation of the low-lying islands. Dry conditions began about 1705 on Boa Vista and Maio, and somewhat earlier on Sal. Sal was evacuated about 1705, then repopulated about 1708, only to be evacuated again a little later. Cattle on Boa Vista were almost completely wiped out at the worst of

3

the famine, but herds began to recover somewhat toward 1721.[6]

c. 1710 Serious famine in the lower valley of the Senegal, killing so many people and cattle that neither the hide trade nor the export of locally manufactured cotton textiles recovered for more than a decade.[7]

1723 Low rainfall causing famine in the lower Senegal valley and eastward through Bambuhu.[8]

1729-31 Low rainfall and famine in Gajaaga, so serious that the slave trade of Fort Saint Joseph was cut back drastically in 1731-32 for lack of millet to keep slaves alive until the high season on the river. The Royal African Company on the Gambia had the same problem in 1731-32 because of an extreme shortage of grain all along the river.[9]

1747-58 A period of low rainfall in Senegambia began about 1747, and famine was general in 1747-50 for the whole of the sahal region, where it killed many people and caused large-scale depopulation. Gajaaga alone recovered in 1750; conditions for 1751 not reported; but drought and famine came again in 1752 for the whole length of the Senegal from Gajaaga to the ocean. Many of the slaves awaiting shipment in Saint Louis began to die of starvation and disease. Then, with the high season of 1753, the Senegal rose so far that it flooded half of Saint Louis and washed away part of Fort Saint Joseph in Gajaaga. Some recovery is reported for 1754 and 1755, though the Wolof attempt to rebuild family and village grain stores in 1755 forced the French post in Saint Louis to import some 245 metric tons of millet from Gajaaga, where supplies were better. Then in 1757-58, the rains were again insufficient on the lower Senegal. When the English blockade cut off maritime imports of food for Saint Louis, the French drove away some 500 of the slaves they were holding for shipment rather than see them starve in the fort. ·This is probably the "seven years" of drought remembered in Kaarta and the sahal generally as the *solo*.[10]

1786 Locally low rainfall in the south-bank region of the Gambia and the hinterland of the "southern rivers."[11]

1812 Bad rainfall and famine conditions in Jolof, Waalo, and Kajor—most serious in Jolof.[12]

1833-37 Famine in Fuuta Tooro, beginning with a failure of the rains in 1833, followed by low crests on the Senegal in 1834 and 1835, depressing the quantity of *waalo* land available for cultivation.[13]

1846-53 Period of generally uncertain harvests on the upper Senegal, beginning with low rainfall in 1846 in Bundu, creating famine conditions there by the end of the year. Rains were then low in Fuuta and Bundu alike in 1847. They recovered in 1848-50, but no rain fell in Gajaaga between July 6 and August 20, 1851, the heart of the normal rainy season, and general famine conditions on the Atlantic Coast and all along the river set in with a second failure of the rains in 1852. In 1853, moisture was adequate near the coast, but not in Gajaaga. Meanwhile, the French fed the garrisons in Gajaaga with millet imported from Wolof country.[14]

A CHRONICLE OF DROUGHT AND FAMINE IN THE NIGER BEND, 1617-1771[15]

1616-17 Niger flood in 1616 followed by drought in 1617.
1639-43 The great famine of the seventeenth century, 1639 and
  1643 virtually without rain, and low rainfall in intervening
  years.
1669-70 Famine from two successive very dry years.
1695-   Famine, most severe in vicinity of Timbuktu.
1704 Flood followed by a drought and famine.
1721-22 Drought and famine.
1738-56 Worst famine reported. Killed about half the population
  of Timbuktu and parts of the Niger bend. Forced evacuation of
  some regions and of some desert oasis towns.
1770-71 Famine and drought in Timbuktu.

A PARTIAL CHRONICLE OF LOCUST PLAGUES AND MAJOR
EPIDEMICS IN SENEGAMBIA, 1574-1869

1574 or before Probably within preceding two or three decades,
  a major plague of locusts and famine in Kajor, but not affecting the Cape Verde Islands, which were the primary source of
  relief supplies.[16]
23 January 1606 A cloud of red locusts darkened the sky at
  Portudal, eating all vegetation.[17]
1641 A plague of locusts on the Senegambian coast.[18]
1724 A smallpox epidemic on the Gambia.[19]
1750 Locusts in the hinterland of Cacheu and along the lower
  Gambia.[20]
1758 Locusts destroyed the millet crop in Waalo, but not in
  Kajor.[21]
1750-58 Yellow fever epidemics attacked the European posts in 1750,
  1759, 1764, 1766, 1769, and 1778. The epidemic of 1778 killed
  more than 80 per cent of the Europeans on Gorée at the time.[22]
1786 Locusts (along with drought) caused a famine south of the
  Gambia.[23]
1835-36 Smallpox epidemic in the middle valley of the Senegal.[24]
1868-69 The great cholera epidemic in Senegambia, with low death
  rates among European residents, but mortality rates variable
  between about 140 and 280 per thousand among the African population.[25]

SOURCES

1. F. Mauro, *Le Portugal et l'Atlantique au xviie siècle
(1570-1670): Etude économique* (Paris, 1960), p. 166; W. Rodney,
"Portuguese Attempts at Monopoly on the Upper Guinea Coast, 1580-
1650," *JAH*, 6:307-22 (1965); J. Barbot, *A Description of the
Coasts of North and South Guinea* (n.p., 1732), p. 32.
  2. Chambonneau, "Deux textes sur le Sénégal (1673-1677)," ed.
C. I. A. Ritchie, *BIFAN-B*, 30:289-353 (1968), p. 352.
  3. Barbot, *Guinea*, p. 32.

4. La Courbe, *Premier voyage du Sieur de la Courbe fait à la coste d'Afrique en 1865*, ed. Pierre Cultru (Paris, 1913), p. 79.

5. Hodges to RAC, 16 September 1690, printed in T. G. Stone, "The Journey of Cornelius Hodges in Senegambia," *English Historical Review*, 39:89-95 (1924), p. 91.

6. G. Roberts [pseud.], *Four Years of Voyages of Captain George Roberts* ... (London, 1726), pp. 386-87.

7. Saint-Robert to CI, 8 March 1721, ANF, C6 6.

8. Du Bellay to CI, 25 May 1824, ANF, C6 8; Levens, Report to CI, 10 July 1725, BN, FF, NA, 9339, f. 42.

9. Boucard to CI, 1 April 1732, BN, FF, NA, 9341; Rogers to RAC, 25 April 1732, T 70/7.

10. P. Marty, trans., "Les chroniques de Oualata et de Néma," *Revue des études islamiques*, 1:355-426, 531-75 (1927), p. 565; Conseil du Sénégal to CI, 3 June 1754, ANF, C6 14; Conseil du Sénégal to CI, 15 March 1756, CO 267/12; Le Bart to Compagnie du Sénégal, Malaga, 30 November 1756, ANF, C6 14; J. Tufton Mason, despatch of 22 December 1758, Fort Lewis, CO 267/12; C. Monteil, "Le coton chez les noirs," *CEHSAOF*, 11:585-684 (1926).

11. William Littleton, Evidence to House of Commons Committee on the Slave Trade, 18 June 1789, *Accounts and Papers*, 25 (635), p. 206.

12. MacCarthy to Bathurst, 13 August 1813, CO 267/36, and 21 February 1814, CO 267/38.

13. D. Robinson, P. Curtin, and J. Johnson, "A Tentative Chronology of Fuuta Tooro from the Sixteenth through the Nineteenth Centuries," *CEA*, 12:555-92 (1972), table 11.

14. A. Raffenel, *Nouveau voyage au pays des nègres*, 2 vols. (Paris, 1856), 1:34; Robinson and others, "Chronology," pp. 586-87; André, fils, to Governor, Senudebu, 15 January 1848, ANS, 13 G 245; Commandant Bakel to Ordonnateur, 20 August 1850, ANS, 13 G 176; E. Saulnier, *La compagnie de Galam au Sénégal* (Paris, 1921), pp. 172, 174; Rey to Governor, 25 June 1853, ANS, 13 G 166.

15. Sékéné Mody Cissoko, "Famines et épidémiques à Tombouctou et dans la boucle du Niger du xvie au xviiie siècle," *BIFAN*, 30:806-21 (1968).

16. A. Alvares d'Almada, *Tratado breve dos rios de Guine de Cabo Verde*, reedited by Luis Silveira (1594; Lisbon, 1946).

17. P. van den Broeck, "Voiages de Pierre van den Broeck au Cap vert, à Angola, et aux Indes orientales," in R. A. C. Renneville, ed., *Recueil des voiages qui ont servi à l'établissement et aux progrès de la Compagnie des Indes Orientales*, 5 vols. (Amsterdam, 1703-10), 4:307.

18. J. Ogilby, *Africa* (London, 1670), p. 98.

19. Extract of Plunkitt to RAC, 19 November 1724, T 70/7.

20. M. Adanson, *Voyage to Senegal* (London, 1759), p. 159; W. Rodney, *A History of the Upper Guinea Coast 1545-1800* (Oxford, 1970), p. 101.

21. J. Tufton Mason despatch of 22 December 1758, from Fort Lewis, CO 267/12.

22. L. Jore, "Les établissements français sur la côte occidentale d'Afrique de 1758 à 1809," *RFHC*, 51:267;

George Grant to Africa Committee, 7 January 1765, CO 388/52.

23. Littleton, Evidence to Commons Committee on the Slave Trade, p. 206.

24. Bujol to MC, 23 February 1836, ANS, 2 B 16.

25. Robert Waters, Report of 4 June 1869, PP, xliii (140), pp. 15-17; A. Beaumier, "Le choléra au Maroc, sa marche au Sahara jusqu'au Sénégal en 1868," *Bulletin de la Société de géographie de Paris,* 3 (6th ser.):281-305 (1872), pp. 287-300.

2 | SUMMARY OF FRENCH REGULATIONS APPLYING TO THE TRADE OF SENEGAMBIA

This checklist summarizes the major changes in the French regulations governing the French slave trade from Senegambia. Unless otherwise noted, the data are from P. Cultru, *Les origines de l'Afrique occidentale: Histoire du Sénégal du xve siècle à 1870* (Paris, 1910), pp. 264-65.

Up to 1672 slaves were furnished to the French West Indies
  mainly by the Dutch and English, though the trade of 1664-72
  was a legal monopoly of the Compagnie des Indes Occidentales.
1672-75 The slave trade was open to any French shipper, and
  each received a bounty of 10 livres tournois (about £0.78
  sterling at the time) on each slave landed in the French
  Caribbean.
1675-79 A legal monopoly was granted to Jean Oudiette, a
  French tax farmer.
1679-84 The legal monopoly was transferred to the Compagnie
  du Sénégal, which promised in return to import 2,000 slaves a
  year to the French Antilles. It failed to meet the agreement.
1684 The monopoly was transferred to the Compagnie de Guinée,
  on its promise to deliver 1,000 slaves a year, which it too
  failed to accomplish.
1696 A Nouvelle Compagnie du Sénégal took over the monopoly
  and again failed to deliver the promised number of slaves.
  (The period 1673-96 is covered in Abdoulaye Ly, *La Compagnie
  du Sénégal* [Paris, 1958].)
1701-13 The Compagnie de l'Asiente (the *asiento,* in Spanish,
  took over the contract for delivery of slaves to Spanish
  America. It also failed to deliver.
1713-16 The slave trade was opened to any French shipper who
  would pay a duty of 30 livres (£1.51) per slave imported into
  Saint Domingue and 25 livres (£1.26) for each slave imported
  into the French Windward Islands.
1716-20 Trade remained open, but only to shippers from Rouen,

La Rochelle, Bordeaux, Nantes, and Saint Malo, and for a reduced duty of 20 livres per slave (£0.70 at the average exchange of 1719).

1720-25 The monopoly was again granted, this time to the Compagnie des Indes, on the promise that it would deliver 30,000
slaves to Saint Domingue over a twenty-five-year period. This
promise too was unfulfilled.

1725 The monopoly was regranted to a new Compagnie des Indes,
which in turn sold its monopoly privilege piecemeal to private
shippers for a fee of 20 livres per slave (£0.80 par value),
while the company itself also received bounty from the French
Crown of 13 livres (£0.52) for each slave exported.

1758 The Compagnie des Indes lost its privilege with the loss
of Saint Louis to the English in 1758, though the French kept
Gorée. The slave trade was then opened to all French shipping,
and a bounty of 100 livres (£3.98) was paid for each slave de-
livered to the French Antilles, a bounty raised to 160 livres
(£6.37) in 1787.

1774 A new "Compagnie de Commerce en Afrique" was chartered,
principally for the gum trade north of the Senegal. It was
based in Le Havre, and had special privileges at the French
government post at Gorée. (Jore, *Etablissements français*, pp.
320-28).

1776-77 The company was renamed the Compagnie de Guiane and
given land grants and other privileges in French Guiana, along
with exclusive rights to the French trade from Cape Verde to
the Casamance River. It also received a bounty of 150 livres
each (£4.80) for the first 1,200 slaves landed in Cayenne and
100 livres each (£3.20) for the second 1,200. ("Questions
relatives à la Compagnie de Guiane," ANF, C6 18.)

1784 The Compagnie de Guiane lost its monopoly over all commodities other than gum, but that monopoly was extended for a further nine years.

1786 The company was rechartered as the Compagnie du Sénégal and
again endowed with a legal monopoly over the trade in slaves,
gold dust, ivory, and beeswax from the Senegal River, in return
for assuming the cost of maintaining the French forts and factories in Senegambia. (P. Dardel, *Navires et marchandises dans
les ports de Rouen et du Havre au xviiie siècle* (Paris, 1963),
pp. 413-35; Jore, *Etablissements français*, pp. 329-35; "Aperçu
pour la Compagnie du Sénégal," unsigned and undated memorandum
in ANF, C6 20.)

1789 The Company's monopoly was extended to the trade of Gorée
and the coast between Gorée and the Gambia River, inclusive.

1791 In January, the Compagnie du Sénégal was suppressed by the
Constituent Assembly, leaving the trade of Senegambia legally
open to any French citizen.

3 | CHRONOLOGICAL OUTLINES OF GAJAAGA (GALAM OR GADIAGA)

        One problem implicit in a study of one country's history seen through another country's archives is the fact that the yield in relevant data is low. Most European archival collections dealing with Africa tell about European activities, while the much richer African oral traditions are almost always very weak on chronology. Synchronisms like the name of the ruler in a nearby kingdom who was contemporary with a particular event can often be useful clues to chronological tangles, yet a full archival search very far afield from a narrow research area is often simply too time-consuming to be possible.
  One step toward solving this problem is to publish outline chronologies of particular African states or regions. An article already published by D. Robinson, J. Johnson, and myself on the chronology of Fuuta Tooro (in *CEA*, 12:555-92 [1972]) can serve as an example. The expected contribution is not an outline history of the kingdom, merely a notice of the dates of public events like battles, wars, or the movements of individuals into and out of office. While the chronology of western Senegambian history is being independently investigated by Boubacar Barry, Jean Boulègue, and others (see bibliography), that of northeastern Senegal has not received so much attention. The summaries here and in appendices 7-9 are designed partly to help fill this gap. The chronology of drought, locust plagues, and epidemic disease in appendix 1 is also relevant, though it will not be repeated here for each individual country.

1686 Tunka reported as Maxã ("Maza" or "Maca," usually "Makhan" today) of the town of "Boubé Segalle" (above Tafasirga and be-low Dramane).[1]
1686-90 French ran fleets to Gajaaga each high season.[2]
1698 Bruë began a new series of annual French voyages to Gajaaga, and the French built a fort in about 1699 at Dramane, which they evacuated December 1702. Maxã was still alive and

claimed the office of Tunka, but against the counter-claims of a certain Bukari of "Bournaguy," a place identified as being at 14°17' north, and downstream from "Tafasiga" (a contradiction if the reference is to the modern Tafasirga at 14°45' north).[3]

1707 The French attempted to reestablish a post in Gajaaga, but the expedition sent for that purpose was forced back to the coast by illness.[4]

1710 French reestablished trade to Gajaaga, this time at Maxaana, where they built Fort Saint Joseph, completed in 1714.[5] Tunka Ñame ("Niamé") was in office, and his *alquier*, Badel (the official in charge of stranger traders), was also a key figure.[6]

1719 Ñame and Badel were still important, but Maxã of Tambukaane also claimed the Tunkaship, and Seega Dua of Xaaso (Khasso) claimed a general suzerainty over Gajaaga. In Maxaana, Amadi Kane ("Amadi Canay") was just proclaimed Tunka of the town. Another nearby power was Mahamad "Labe" of the Haire ("Ahéré") Moors, and a Moroccan army was also operating in the vicinity.[7]

1722 War broke out between the French post and Maxaana, in which the French attacked Maxaana, sacked the town, and drove away Amadi Kane, its Tunka. Moroccans appeared on the north bank, having already forced the Haire Moors to pay tribute (October).[8]

1723 Juula negotiated with the English on the Gambia, holding out hope of large trade to Gajaaga and offering to take a European inland with them. Late in 1723 or early in 1724, Bambuk people raided Tambukaane.[9]

1724 A Moroccan army arrived in mid-April, operating in conjunction with a second Futaanke force under Samba Gelaajo Jegi, who stayed for a time at the French fort at Maxaana and left his family there in his absence. On June 4 and 5, the two armies marched along the river in two divisions, sacking and plundering the villages of Gunjuru ("Gonguiro"), "Gongallé," Tambukaane ("Tambaucany"), Ambideeji ("Ambidery"), "Golmi ("Gagny"), and "Macayamaré." The commander of this force was the tenth commander of Ormankoobe sent out from Morocco. The captives taken in these raids were ransomed for a price of 19,500 gros or 13,000 mithqals of gold (approximate weight, 74.57 kgs).

In late June, the Moroccans departed for raids into Bambuhu and Bundu, and people from Bambuhu began counter-raids on Gajaaga towns and villages. French relations with Gajaaga deteriorated sharply, since the Soninke believed that the French were responsible for inviting both the Moroccans and Samba Gelaajo Jegi to Gajaaga.

The raids, combined with the effects of a recent famine, reduced the population of Gajaaga to about one-quarter of its size in 1719 before the troubles began, though many who had taken flight might someday return.[10]

1725 Tunka Ñame died. In May, a brief war took place between the French and the Baacili, the French in this case deriving at least moral support from the clerical towns of Gajaaga.[11]

1730 A more important war between the French and the Baacili broke out, lasted at least into early 1731, and may have been continuous with a new crisis in 1732. The French called this war the Baacili war.[12]

1732 Sieur Pelays, French commandant of Fort Saint Joseph, went insane and claimed to be "king of Galam." Some clerics of the Draame family of Dramane assassinated him.[13]

1733 Tumaane Ñakalel (Niakalel) of Farabana and the Saatigi Maxã of Samarina (both small states in Bambuhu) came to make peace with the Gajaaga towns and to ask the French to set up factories in their states. Peace with Bambuhu was arranged, but the French continued to be chronically at war with some factions of the Baacili, though supported by the clerical towns.[14]

1735-36 Sieur Garnier acted in a high-handed manner in dealing with the Baacili in matters of customs payments; they assassinated him 23 December 1735, and the French found themselves isolated from the Baacili and the clerics alike, and trade cut off, at least through 1736. Yuuba Jaalo (Ayuba Diallo) was captured and kept in irons at Fort Saint Joseph from 6 June 1736 to early 1737.[15] At this period Muusa was still Tunka of Gajaaga, but the most important Baacili leader was Alimana.

1737 Tunka Muusa was deposed, and Bukari Setei of Maxaana was installed in his place as Tunka of all Gajaaga.[16]

1737-38 Gajaaga favored Konko Bubu Muusa as Saatigi of Fuuta, but the pretender Samba Gelaajo Jegi received French support as part of a French-made alliance consisting of Samba Gelaajo, a band of Ormankoobe who had been lately raiding toward Bambara country, and the Brakna Moors. The military operations began with a combined Moorish-Samba Gelaajo sack of Dramane and some other Gajaaga towns. Samba Gelaajo's ultimate invasion of Fuuta took place in March 1738.[17]

1741-42 A period of comparative peace and good trade prevailed in Gajaaga, when local politics was dominated by the rivalry of Alimana (of Maxaana) and Jabe Tambo (or Tambukaane) for leadership.[18]

1744-45 or possibly late in 1743. Civil war broke out between the supporters of Alimana and Jabe Tambo and continued at least through September 1745.[19]

1751 War with Xaaso had been in progress for some time, damping down the internal rivalry among the Baacili. The two factions were now led by Alimana and Bukoma, the son of Jabe Tambo, who had died sometime between 1745 and 1751. By the latter part of 1751, the situation was complicated by the appearance of Sule Njai, a contestant for the office of Saatigi of Fuuta Tooro, now in *fergo* after a defeat. He tried to mount an expedition against Bundu, where his old enemy Eliman Maka Jiiba was still in office. The Masasi leaders of the Bambara who were to settle in Kaarta first appeared in the east at about this time. They were allied with Xaaso against Gajaaga, to begin with, but then began raids into Xaaso as well. They were known in Gajaaga as the "black Ormankoobe."[20]

1752-58 This was a period of declining trade, and of prolonged

war with Xaaso and with Bundu a part of the time. In early
stages, the Bambara were on the side of Gajaaga, but they
dropped out after a time. The chronic war stopped the caravans
coming through from the east, and the slave trade to Fort Saint
Joseph nearly stopped, in spite of efforts to keep it going by
hiring Moors to protect caravans, and, after 1756, paying the
Xasoonke leaders for not raiding passing caravans.[21]

1757-62 Because of wartime conditions, French began a gradual
evacuation of their post in Gajaaga. In the high season of
1757, they sent up river only food for the garrison. In 1759,
they evacuated the commandant and all but twenty-two of the
former staff and garrison. The British evacuated the remaining French in 1760, and then evacuated their own people in 1762
because of high mortality. This ended the regular occupation
of a European post in Gajaaga until 1818.[22]

1758 The selection of a new Tunka was contested briefly, but one
was chosen and Gajaaga was reunited. The French records mention
no names.[23]

1762 Siliman, the Tunka of Maxaana, seized control of the empty
Fort Saint Joseph with its cannon and made himself an independent power, no longer under a Tunka for Gajaaga as a whole but
in complete control of Maxaana and some nearby villages.
Siliman had been educated in Saint Louis, spoke both English
and French, and had a Wolof wife who claimed to be a Christian.[24]

1765 The Tunkaship of Maxaana, with its control over the fort,
had now passed to Samba Kongol,[25] who may be tentatively identified as the father of Samba Xumba Jaama and Samba Yaasin,
the rivals for power in Gajaaga in the 1830's and 1840's.

1779 French sent a government expedition to Gajaaga following
their reoccupation of Saint Louis, the first European company
or government expedition up the Senegal since 1762, but they
did not reoccupy the fort.[26] (The absence of European residents in Gajaaga in 1762-1818 accounts for the very sparse
documentary record of that period.)

1785 The chief of Bakel town was Adami Conkoli ("Adami Thion-
coli").[27]

1801 or possibly early 1802. Bundu forced Gajaaga to cede
part of the south bank of the Senegal, from the mouth of the
Faleme downstream nearly to Bakel.[28]

1810's A period of political turmoil, based in large part on the
drive of Kaarta for greater power and influence on the upper
Senegal and its intervention in the affairs of Gajaaga, Bundu,
Xaaso, and Fuuta. The usual alignment early in the decade was
Fuuta and Bundu against Kaarta and Gajaaga.

1815-19 A major war began with a Kaartan demand of tribute from
Bundu. Early in 1817, Bundu, allied with Xaaso, invaded Kaarta
simultaneously with a Kaartan invasion of Bundu that passed
through Gajaaga. The Bunduunke army, however, returned and
routed the Kaartans at Bulebane, capital of Bundu. In early
1818, Bundu laid seige to Tambukaane in Gajaaga, but its forces
were driven off by a Kaartan army. Lower Gajaaga (or Goi) and
Fuuta Tooro then joined on the Bunduunke side, and they fought
a major battle against Kaarta in April 1818, in Gajaaga. The

Bunduunke-Futaanke forces lost, retreated into Fuuta, and decided to sue for peace, which was arranged during the dry
season of 1818-19. At this time, Bundu was the strongest state
in the vicinity, with the possible exception of Kaarta. It
controlled Kuñani ("Kounguel") and Bakel (along with a strip
of about 10 kms along the south bank of the Senegal between the
two towns). Gidimaxa on the north bank was tributary to
Kaarta. The Tunka of all Gajaaga was Samba Kongol of Maxaana,
a leader who had been to Saint Louis and knew French.[29]

1818 The first French expedition up the Senegal since the reoccupation of Saint Louis reached Gajaaga in September and established a temporary post at Bakel in December.[30]

1820 The French commission to investigate the upper Senegal decided upon Bakel as the best permanent French post.[31]

1821 In January, a new Tunka was chosen for Gajaaga. In May, a
group of men having the support of the Tunka of Tiyaabu tried
to assassinate the French commander at Bakel and did kill another French official. This led to a short war in which the
Njaibe of Bakel and the Bundunkoobe sided with the French a-
gainst Tiyaabu.[32]

1824 An unnamed Tunka of Gajaaga died.[33] The Tunka of Tiyaabu
was Sili, a senile old man.

1825 A new Tunka was chosen for Gajaaga. Samba Yaasin of Maxaana
and Samba Xumba Jaama of Tiyaabu were mentioned for the first
time as important people in Gajaaga.[34]

1827 The villages of Yafera and Kuñani, theoretically belonging
to Bakel, were occupied by people from Gidimaxa whom Bakel
could not remove, though the people were persuaded to remove
themselves peacefully early in 1828.

The unnamed Tunka of Gajaaga died, and a new Tunka was chosen.
In August, the old quarrel between the French fort and the
Baacili of Tiyaabu, concerning customs payments, flared up
again. This time, the French shelled Tiyaabu and held Samba
Kongol as a prisoner in Saint Louis for a few months.[35]

1828 Samba Kongol of Tiyaabu tried to assassinate M. Velentin,
the local manager of the Galam Company. Samba Yaasin of Maxaana
made difficulties for French shipping seeking to pass Maxaana,
but his own position in Kamera (or upper Gajaaga) was threatened
by an alliance of other leaders, including Suraxe Fatima.[36]

1829 Kuñani, occupied by the Njai of Bakel, was threatened by
the Baacili of Tiyaabu, but the Njai had the support of Gidimaxa
and Bundu as well as the French. Gidimaxa and Bundu needed a
non-Baacili-controlled town for the sake of keeping open their
millet trade across the Senegal.[37]

1830 The Tunka of Tiyaabu was Bubu.[38]

1833 The Tunka of Tiyaabu died. He was Tunka of Gajaaga as well,
which meant that he collected two different payments from the
French—one as Tunka of Gajaaga and the other as Tunka of Tiyaabu. But then Samba Xumba Jaama succeeded as Tunka of Tiyaabu
only, the Tunkaship of Gajaaga passing to Jaji of Kotere. Jaji
was very old, and he moved to Maxaana, where Samba Yaasin was
Tunka of the town. This meant that Samba Yaasin began to col-
lect Jaji's customs as well as his own. This was the beginning

of de facto division of Gajaaga into Goi (lower) and Kamera (upper), and the beginning of the "War of the Two Sambas."[39]

1834 Samba Yaasin of Maxaana raised a Kamera and Bambara army and attacked Tiyaabu by surprise, capturing the city and killing all the Baacili there; but Samba Xumba Jaama was in Bakel that day, so that he was able to escape to Fuuta.

1835 Samba Xumba Jaama and his son Sili returned from Fuuta and established themselves in Kuñani rather than trying to rebuild Tiyaabu. A French gunboat attacked Maxaana and forced a settlement on Samba Yaasin on French terms.[40]

1836 Duranton, a French trader and son-in-law of the king of Xaaso, moved his operations to Kuñani after his first establishment in Xaaso had been sacked by the Bambara. Samba Xumba Jaama then stopped a vessel of the Galam Company from passing Kuñani on its way to Maxaana,[41] and sporadic fighting broke out between the Baacili of Kuñani and the Njai of Bakel.

1837 Duranton visited Bakel on June 24. When the commander of the post demanded that he surrender three cannon and some other arms he had brought down from Xaaso, he refused and was immediately arrested on charges of furnishing arms to Samba Xumba Jaama and aiding English trade to the Gambia. Later in the year, Samba Yaasin again began raiding into Goi with Bambara troops, and Samba Xumba Jaama continued sporadic fighting against Bakel.

In August, the steamer *Africain* went up from Saint Louis and after a show of force,[42] forced new treaties on the two Sambas.

1839 Tunka Jaji died, but even earlier, on July 2, Samba Xumba Jaama had seized the ship carrying the customs payments to Maxaana. The French threatened force against Samba Xumba Jaama to get restitution.

Meanwhile, Samba Yaasin formed an entente with Bundu and Kaarta with the understanding that all three would send their commerce through to the Gambia rather than deal with the French, a situation that continued into ...

1840 but the war of the Sambas tended to quiet down to an undeclared truce as the French gave more support to Samba Xumba Jaama and stopped paying customs to Samba Yaasin.[43]

1841 Samba Yaasin died between 20 September 1840 and 20 January 1842—probably in 1841. Samba Xumba Jaama became Tunka of Goi, while the Tunkaship of Kamera was contested between Tambu, brother of Samba Yaasin, and Barka, son of Samba Yaasin. The French recognized Tambu and paid half the annual Gajaaga customs to Tambu, and the other half to Samba Xumba Jaama.[44]

1842 Bundu attacked Maxaana and Tambukaane.[45]

1845 A general peace conference of the important Baacili was held January 23-25, at the suggestion of Paul Holle and Zeler of Saint Louis. The conference was concerned mainly about conflict in Kamera over the distribution of the French customs payments, and it decided to divide them between the chiefs of Maxaana and Suraxe Fatima, chief of Lani (Lanel) and Gucube (Gouthioubé).

The war between Kamera and Goi meanwhile continued through the remainder of the year, marked principally by a joint attack

on Maxaana in October mounted by Goi and Bundu together, an
attack which was repulsed.[46]

1846 The quarrel over the Kamera customs and their distribution
continued. Paul Holle, the commandant in Bakel, stopped payments to Suraxe, while Suraxe declared that no French shipping
would be allowed to pass Gucube bound up the Senegal, or to
pass up the Faleme. Bundu and Goi, still enemies of Maxaana,
declared that any French action against Suraxe that involved
the help of Maxaana would automatically bring them into the
war on the opposite side. The French then embarked on deli-
cate diplomacy to assure the neutrality of Barka of Maxaana,
while they attacked Suraxe on their own. On December 12 and
13 they shelled Gucube, and a landing party burned a part of
the town.[47]

1847 The Goi and the Maxaana faction each threatened to bring
in Kaarta on its own side, but the French and the Gajaaga clerics acted as mediators and secured a settlement on 31 July 1847
between Barka of Maxaana and Samba Xumba Jaama of Kuñiani.
Suraxe was not a party to the peace settlement, and he was
abandoned by his former allies in Bundu. In the last days of
the year, war between Gidimaxa and all of Gajaaga broke out,
following Gidimaxa raids across the Senegal.[48]

1848 War with Gidimaxa continued. Gidimaxa raided the vicinity
of Bakel on January 24 and Arundu in March. Fuuta joined on
the side of Gajaaga in August. (In 1845-46, Fuuta and Bundu
together had fought Gidimaxa and Kaarta and the Īdaw ꜥAish
Moors, Gidimaxa's suzerain, but Gajaaga had been theoretically
neutral in this war and the only Gajaaga participants had been
some of the Maxaana Baacili.)[49]

   Late in the year, Suraxe again began stopping French shipping,
and he entered the Gajaaga-Gidimaxa war on the side of Gidimaxa.[50]

1849 In late December 1848 or early January 1849, Almaami Saada
of Bundu precipitated a reversal of alliances. Having indicated
that he would join Goi and the French in a renewed attack on
Suraxe at Gucube, he suddenly marched his army into Goi in
January, raiding the countryside around Bakel, Yafera, and
Golmi. At the same time, Suraxe seized the Goi villages of
Arundu and Balu on the lower Faleme. On February 15, peace
was arranged between Bundu and Goi, in which Tunka Samba Xumba
Jaama promised to move his capital from Kuñiani back to Tiyaabu,
and the French promised to pay Bundu 100 pièces de Guinée
(£52.70). But the conditions were not met, and war broke out
again in October, with a renewed Bunduunke invasion of Goi in
December and many scattered Moorish raids into northern Bundu.
Meanwhile, about July, Maxaana forces moved toward Gucube, and
Suraxe was so alarmed that he evacuated the town and sent all
noncombatants to Gidimaxa for safety. In October, the French
then attacked both Gucube and Lani from the river, destroying
Lani.[51]

1850 The Bundu-Gajaaga war continued until March 1850, when the
French managed to act as mediators. Most of the military action was Moorish raids on northern Bundu and Bunduunke raids

into Goi. After the peace, however, the Moors continued to
raid in Goi. The Bundu-Goi peace of March was followed by the
submission of Suraxe to the other Baacili (between March and
June), ratified by a general assembly of all important Baacili
other than Barka of Maxaana (son of Samba Yaasin). The capital
of Goi returned to Tiyaabu. Late in 1850 Suraxe tried to return to his original town of Musaala.[52]

1851 Possibly late in 1850, but more likely in 1851 before October, Suraxe was assassinated by people from Tambukaane. This
left Maxaana dominant in Kamera, with Barka in nominal command
but the real power lying with his younger brother Sule (who had
earlier caused a major political disturbance by killing Amadi
Sina, his maternal uncle).[53]

1852 This was a period of increasing raids from the Moors to the
north, especially the "Asker," and of Futaanke raids against
Moorish caravans. These Futaanke raiders were often based in
Gajaaga towns like Manael or Jawara.

In March, a Bambara army crossing Gajaaga to raid into Fuuta
got into a fight with the Njai of Bakel, and the French fort
was briefly engaged, though full-scale war between Kaarta and
Goi was avoided.[54]

In November, war broke out between Lani and Maxaana.

1853 A persistence of Futaanke raids on the *zwāya* caravans from
bases in Gajaaga was tolerated by the Baacili. The French tried
to meet this problem by pressure on Samba Xumba Jaama, but he
was too old to be effective (and his son, Sili, had only a small
following among the other Baacili). In November, a new civil
war broke out in Kamera, between Lani (which now had the Tunkaship) and Maxaana.[55]

1854 The Tunka from Lani died in early April and was replaced by
a new Tunka from Digokori. He, in turn, was replaced in June
by Wali Samba of Kotera. Persistent Futaanke raids on the Moorish caravans tended to drive the gum trade upstream from Bakel
to Maxaana.

When Farabana in Bambuhu fell to Shaykh Umar Taal, many refugees fled to Maxaana. The sons of a Samba Yaasin refused to
turn them over to Umar in November, and the Umarian army attacked and completely destroyed both Maxaana and Tambukaane,
killing all of Samba Yaasin's sons and taking their women
prisoner.[56]

1855 The destruction of Maxaana terrified those who were not actively for the Umarian revolution, so that Afro-French traders
and the French post were virtually isolated. The only actively
anti-Umarian forces were those of the Īdaw 'Aish Moors and a
few of the Njai from Bakel. In April, the French fort in Bakel
turned its guns on the town and levelled it. In July and
August, waterborne French expeditions destroyed Tiyaabu and
Kuñani. August 9, the French annexed Bakel and appointed Sire
Siliman Njai as village head. In September and October, France
signed treaties with Xaaso, Kamera, and Gidimaxa, each of which
recognized that France was "master of the river" and had a
right to trade freely where it wanted.[57] On December 18 and
19, Kamera resumed the war against the French under the

leadership of the Draame, the clerics of Dramane, who had
been the first to declare their allegiance to Shaykh Umar.

1856 The Franco-Kamera war lasted until June 27. The French
set up a main base at Maxaana, from which they shelled and
burned towns up and down the river, burning Dramane three different times.

In the last week of June, "the old Tunka" of Tiyaabu died
(Samba Xumba Jaama?).[58]

1858 August 19, 1858, Goi signed a treaty with France ceding all
territory between Bakel and the Faleme and placing the remainder under a French protectorate.

1859 Shaykh Umar marched eastward through Gajaaga for the last
time. He attacked the French post at Matam in April, crossing over into Gajaaga about May 1 with a following estimated
at 12,000 to 15,000 people, about 500 horses, and many cattle.
His military force was about 500 cavalry and 4,000 men on
foot, armed with firearms. He fought a short action against
the French near Bakel but made no frontal attack on the fort
(May 5 and 7). Crossing to the north bank at Jagili (opposite
Kuñani) on May 10, he moved on upstream to Solu, opposite
Kotera, where he remained until May 18. Then he sent his noncombatants east to Kaarta and took his military into Gidimaxa,
where he captured Gemu without a fight. Meanwhile, another
force of some 3,000 Futaanke and Gidimaxa in Umar's service
tried to capture Arundu and failed. They then moved on and
captured both Dramane and Maxaana.[58]

SOURCES

1. J. Labat, *Nouvelle relation de l'Afrique occidentale*, 4
vols. (Paris, 1728), 3:308-9.

2. Chambonneau, "Relation du Sr. Chambonneau," *Bulletin de
géographie historique et descriptive*, 2:308-21 (1898); C. Hodges
to RAC, 16 September 1690, printed in Stone, "Journey of Cornelius Hodges," p. 94.

3. Labat, *Nouvelle relation*, 4:22-31.

4. John Snow to RAC, 9 August 1707, T 70/5.

5. Labat, *Nouvelle relation*, 4:30; La Courbe to CI, 30 June
1710, ANF, C6 3.

6. Bruë to Collé, 9 December 1716, ANF, C6 5, or copy in BN,
FF, NA, 9341.

7. Bruë to Violaine, 23 October 1719, ANF, C6 5, or copy in
BN, FF, NA, 9341.

8. Charpentier to CI, 12 October 1722, Saint-Robert to CI,
28 December 1722, ANF, C6 7; Charpentier, Memoir of 1 April 1723,
ANF, C6 10.

9. Orfeur to RAC, 6 June 1723, T 70/7; Charpentier, Procès
verbal of 31 March 1724, ANF C6 7.

10. ANF, C6 7 passim, esp. Charpentier memoranda of 20 June
1724 and 1 April 1725; Levens, memoranda of 10 and 19 July 1725,
ANF, C6 9, or copy in BN, FF, NA, 9339, f. 144.

11. Levens, Report of 10 July 1725, ANF, C6 9.

12. Boucard to CI, Fort Saint-Joseph, 1 April 1732, ANF, C6 10, or copy in BN, FF, NA, 9341.

13. De Louard de Beaufort to Devaulx, Galam, 29 January 1733, ANF, C6 10.

14. Devaulx to CI, 14 May and 4 September 1733, and De Louard de Beaufort to Levens, Fort Saint-Joseph, 3 March 1733, ANF, C6 10.

15. Saint-Adon to CI, 2 December 1736, ANF, C6 11.

16. Saint-Adon to CI, 20 April 1737, ANF, C6 11.

17. Saint-Adon to CI, 20 April 1737, and Devaulx to CI, 20 March 1737 and 15 February 1738, ANF, C6 11; Conseil du Sénégal to CI, 14 May 1738, ANF, C6 11.

18. Boucard to CI, 30 July 1741 and 1 July 1752, ANF, C6 12.

19. Conseil du Sénégal to CI, 28 April 1744, and David to CI, 9 September 1745, ANF, C6 12. These events in Gajaaga will be much clarified with the publication of Pierre David, *Journal d'un voiage fait en bambouc en 1744* (Paris, 1974), ed. André Delcourt.

20. Conseil du Sénégal to CI, 20 August 1751 and 24 February 1752, ANF, C6 13.

21. Conseil du Sénégal to CI, 25 July 1752, ANF, C6 13; Conseil du Sénégal to CI, 15 March 1756, CO 267/12; Le Bart to CI, 30 November 1747, ANF, C6 14; Conseil du Sénégal to CI, 3 October 1757, CO 267/12; Conseil du Sénégal to CI, 2 March 1747, ANF C6 14. (The French despatches bearing English Colonial Office file numbers were captured by the English and filed along with other correspondence from English Senegal.)

22. Aussenac to CI, 8 January 1759, ANF, C6 14; J. Tufton Mason, despatch of 27 December 1758, CO 267/12; Richard Worge, despatch of 19 October 1759, CO 267/12; Joseph Debat to R. Worge, James Fort, no date but c. late 1762, T 70/30.

23. Conseil du Sénégal to CI, 6 April 1758, CO 267/12.

24. Saugnier, *Relations de plusieurs voyages à la côte d' Afrique, à Maroc, au Sénégal, à Gorée, à Galam...* (Paris, 1791), pp. 210, 214-15; D. H. Lamiral, *L'Affrique et le peuple affriquain* (Paris, 1789), pp. 329-30.

25. Return dated 16 March 1765, CO 388/52.

26. Gauthier de Chevigny to Governor, c. October 1779, ANF, Marine, B4 149.

27. Saugnier, *Voyages*, p. 223.

28. Laserre to MC, 16 February 1802, ANF, C6 21.

29. W. Gray, *Travels in Western Africa in the Years 1818, 19, 20 and 21* (London, 1825), pp. 200-207; Duchastelu to Fleuriau, Kuñani, 5 November 1818, ANF-OM, Sénégal IV 15.

30. P. Marty, *Etudes Sénégalaises* (Paris, n.d. [c. 1926]), pp. 118-21, 130.

31. A detailed report of the commission is found in ANS, 1 G 3.

32. Gray, *Western Africa*, p. 282: Hesse to Governor, 7 May 1821, ANS, 13 G 164.

33. Chenaux, "Notes et renseignements laissées," Bakel, 26 August 1825, ANS, 13 G 164.

34. Grout de Beaufort to Governor, 20 January 1825, ANS, 1 G 7.

35. Lelieur de Ville-sur-Acre, report of 13 March 1828,

Governor to Gerardin, 16 July 1828, and Jubelin to Gerardin, 16 July 1828, ANF-OM, Sénégal IV 15.

36. Duranton to Governor, Médine, 30 November 1828, ANS, 1 G 8.

37. Governor to Chenaux, 13 July 1829, ANF-OM, Sénégal IV 15.

38. Commandant Bakel to Governor, 30 August 1830, ANS, 13 G 164.

39. A. Raffenel, *Voyage dans l'Afrique occidentale exécuté en 1843 et 1844* (Paris, 1846), pp. 292-94; L. Flize, "Le Ndiambour et le Gadiaga (Provinces du Sénégal)," *Revue coloniale*, 17 (2nd ser.):390-98 (1857), p. 394.

40. F. Carrère and P. Holle, *De la Sénégambia française* (Paris, 1855), pp. 141-43; Malavois to MC, no. 160, 11 August 1826, ANS, 2 B 16. Recorded oral traditions concerning the war are in CC, Sassana Sissoko, T6 (2), and Samani Sy, T4 (1).

41. Duranton to Governor, 31 August 1827, ANF-OM, Sénégal III 4; Commandant Bakel to Governor, 22 December 1836, 12 Jan. 1837 and 5 July 1837, ANS, 13 G 164.

42. Commandant Bakel to Governor, 6 July 1837, ANS, 13 G 164; Guillet to Soret, note supplementaire, 4 October 1837, ANS, 13 G 22; Guillet to MC, no. 25, 2 November 1837, ANS, 2 B 17; Simon (commander of *Africain*) to Governor, 25 August 1837, ANF, Sénégal IV 15.

43. Charmasson to Commandant Bakel, 3 February 1840, 21 April 1840, 25 May 1840, ANS, 13 G 204; Bouët, "Extrait des notes," September 1840, ANF-OM, Sénégal IV 19; Governor Senegal to MC, no. 62, 16 March 1840, no. 249, 15 August 1840, and no. 296, 20 September 1840, ANS, 2 B 18.

44. Montagnies de la Roque to MC, no. 78, 20 January 1842, and no. 377, 30 September 1842, ANS, 2 B 19.

45. Paul Holle to Governor, 17 August and 29 August 1842, ANS, 13 G 164.

46. Thomas, Passation de service, 11 December 1845, ANS, 13 G 22, pp. 70-71. Potin-Patterson to Governor, Senudebu, 1 December 1846, ANS, 13 G 165.

47. Paul Holle to Governor, 7 March 1847, ANS, 13 G 164; enclosures with Gramont to MC, 13 January 1847, ANF-OM, Sénégal IV 19. The affair is also summarized in Raffenel, *Nouveau voyage*, 1:22-30, 42-43, 243-46.

48. De Maricourt to MC, August 1847, ANF-OM, Sénégal IV 19; Hecquard, Report of 30 July 1847, Bakel, ANS, 13 G 165; Paul Holle to Riverdit, Bakel, 25 November 1847 and 7 January 1848, ANS, 1 G 165.

49. Paul Holle to Governor, 19 May 1846, ANS, 13 G 165.

50. Paul Holle to DAE, 20 October, 10 November, 9 December, and 14 December 1848, ANS, 15 G 165.

51. Paul Holle to DAE, 16 January and 20 August 1849, and Rey to Governor, Bakel, 16 December 1849, ANS, 13 G 165; Vebré to Governor, Senudebu, 30 July and 13 October 1849 and 8 January 1850, ANS, 13 G 246. Riverdit's report on the action was enclosed with Baudin to MC, no. 413, 16 October 1849, ANS, 2 B 30.

52. Rey to Governor, 24 January, 9 February, 10 and 31 March, 10 June, and 5 July 1850, ANS, 13 G 165.

53. Dudras to Governor, 27 October 1851, ANS, 13 G 166.

54. Rey to Governor, 9 January, 10 February, 25 March, 2 April,
and 25 December 1852, ANS, 13 G 166.
55. Reported in detail by many despatches from Rey, commandant
at Bakel, in ANS, 13 G 166.
56. N. d'Erneville to Governor, 27 November 1854, and other
despatches in ANS, 13 G 166.
57. Bargone to Governor, 16 April 1855; Parent to Governor,
Bakel, 24 July and 9 August 1855; Bakel proclamation of 9 August
1855, ANS, 13 G 167. Texts of the Gajaaga treaties of 1855 and
1858 are published in Annuaire du Sénégal, 1882, pp. 3-85, 95.
58. The events of the Franco-Kamera war and the final treaty-
signing with both Gajaaga states are reported in detail in despatches from Bakel, Maxaana, and elsewhere on the upper Senegal
in ANS, 13 G 167.

4 | CHRONOLOGICAL OUTLINES OF BAMBUHU (BAMBOUC OR BAMBUK)

13th century Tradition holds that Bambuhu and Gägarä were conquered by one of Sunjaata's generals, but the region later
broke into independent Malinke kingdoms of Bambuhu, Konkadugu,
and Gägarä. Even before that, Bambuhu had been a regional
name, covering an entity of varying size. Gägarä, for example,
is the surviving form of the semimythical Wangara, the source
of gold exports to North Africa.

c. 1550 The Portuguese established a post in Bambuhu near the
source of gold, but many died of disease and the remainder were
expelled by Africans.[1]

1686-87 The French made efforts to reach Bambuhu and the gold
mines by way of the Senegal River.[2]

1689-90 Cornelius Hodges ascended the Gambia to the vicinity of
Ñoholo, then traveled northeast across Bambuhu to Gunjuru in
Gajaaga, crossed the Senegal, and got as far as Lupuru (16 kms
east of Kayes) before being turned back to the Gambia by Gajaaga opposition to his travels. He reported that the mine at
Neteko had been discovered only in 1683, but the country was
still disturbed by serious famine in 1688 and 1689.[3]

1716 Tumaane Ñakalel was the ruler of Farabana, while a certain
Tumaane Tuure acted as protector of the French post established
by this time at Kainura on the Faleme (in territory later part
of Bundu).[4]

1689-1725 A country called Kombordugu or "Combredougou" lay a-
cross the Faleme in what was later to be southeastern Bundu
and the Makana district of Bambuhu. At this same period a
state called Kontu lay on either side of the Faleme to the
north, occupying the river valley roughly between the modern
towns of Dunde on the north and Tombura on the south.[5]

1725 A French project for the forceful conquest of parts of
Bambuhu failed to materialize, but Sieur Levens visited
"Samarina" (probably the later Sirimana?) and Farabana and
made agreements for fortified French posts at each of the two

capitals. The ruler of Samarina was Maxã. French established a post at Farabana a little later (perhaps 1726), but they went on to Samarina only in 1728.[6]

1726 The Xasoonke invaded Sirimana, causing a serious famine.

1728 A French post was established at "Samarinacouta," chief town of Sirimana, under Sieur Payen, 10 November 1728.[7]

1729 Of the many small kingdoms in Bambuhu, three attracted French attention. These were Farabana, still under Tumaane Ñakalel, Sirimana, under Saatigi Maxã, and Ñambia, under Saatigi Muusa.

1730-31 French negotiated separately with Dua, the village chief of Neteko, for the construction of a French fort near the gold workings there, even though Neteko was within the kingdom of Sirimana and the French already had a fort at "Samarinacouta."[8]

1730's Period of frequent raids into Bambuhu by the Ormankoobe.

1734 French evacuated the two fortified posts at Sirimana and Farabana.

c. 1730-34 The son of Tumaane Ñakalel of Farabana traveled to Saint Louis and France for education, the first recorded journey to Europe by a Bambuhu explorer.[9]

1735 Tumaane Ñakalel of Farabana opened diplomatic negotiations with the Royal African Company, through Thomas Hull's visit to Bundu, but heavy Xasoonke raids into Bambuhu in September and October prevented Hull from visiting Farabana and Sirimana as planned.[10]

1737 Tumaane Ñakalel died 15 January 1737 and was succeeded by his son Amadi as king of Farabana.

1744 Sieur David toured Bambuhu and reestablished a small French fortified post at Farabana, but this was not an elaborate fortification, being only 29 meters by 39 meters, with four rooms, each 3 meters square. Amadi Tumaane still ruled.[11]

1747 Period of flourishing trade for Darisalaam (now disappeared from maps, but then located at approximately 14°13' N 12°10' W in the region of Bambuhu later annexed to Bundu), a clerical village having close commercial ties with the English on the Gambia.[12]

1754 War between Bundu and Amadi Tumaane of Farabana.[13]

1757-58 French activity began again, looking toward a French establishment near some of the Bambuhu gold workings, but this effort was cut off by the English capture of Saint Louis in 1758.[14]

1786 War still chronic between Bundu and Farabana, ending in the late 1780's by Bundu annexation of the east bank of the Faleme, the portion now within the Republic of Senegal, and the resettlement of this region by Fuulbe refugees from Fuuta Jaalõ called *hamanaankoobe* (sing. *kamanaanke*).[15]

1791 Samba was the reigning "king of Bambuk" (probably meaning the ruler of Farabana).[16]

1824 Bambara raids from Kaarta cut right across Bambuhu, destroying towns in Bambuhu as well as those further west in Bundu. The Kaartans had the support of Farabana for these raids, but the opposition and resistance of Awa Demba, ruler of Xaaso. Sirimana village (presumably the town earlier called

Samarinacouta) was not fortified at this time, but Sajora,
later to be the chief town of Sirimana, was a large and well-
fortified village. In general, the Bambara raids meant that
the countryside outside defensible places or fortified villages was very nearly uninhabited, and much of the previous
population had fled south into Konkodugu and even as far as
Fuuta Jaalõ.

1825 Bambara raiders destroyed Toronha on the Faleme (opposite
and slightly upstream from the present Sansande) and Borokono
(about 55 kms due east).[17]

1829 Ñagala and other regions of Bambuhu took the side of Logo
(a section of Xaaso) in an attack on Awa Demba of Xaaso. After a near victory in December, the Logo-Bambuhu forces were
routed.[18]

1854 Shaykh Umar marched north from Dingirai through Bambuhu
on his first move north to the upper Senegal. Most of Farabana chose to flee to Maxaana on the river rather than submit.
Umar was thus able to occupy the empty town, which he made into a temporary capital and the base from which he attacked and
destroyed Maxaana.[19]

1855 Umar from his base in Farabana formed an alliance of most
important Bundunkoobe, many Futankoobe, most of Gajaaga, and
some of Bambuhu, to move east for an attack on Xaaso (where
the French fort was begun that year)—and further east toward
Kaarta and Jara.[20]

1856 March-April. Bokar Saada, the anti-Umar pretender to the
Almanate of Bundu, began military operations from a base in the
French fort at Senudebu. Farabana people joined him, when the
town recovered its population after Umar's departure.[21]

1857 The Farabana people led by Bugul were effective allies of
the French and of Bokar Saada in Bundu. In the high water of
1857, the French and their allies moved up the Faleme with artillery support from the steamer *Serpent,* reestablishing the
power of the anti-Umar factions on both sides of the river.

At that time, the French recognized the following political
units and rulers:[22]

State	Ruler
Farabana	Bugul
Ñagala	Bata Mamadu
Tambaura	Pidi
Jebedugu	Fabamba
Konkadugu	not given
Kamanã	not given, but chief of Kenieba in the Bundu portion of Kamanã was Terenan Muusa
Kunjä	Konta Kura
Ñambia	Penda Tumaane
Kankula	Naikale Muusa

1858 In March, Shaykh Umar returned to Bambuhu and Bundu, where
he paused briefly before moving on into Fuuta in May. Bugul
and his followers in Farabana took refuge in Bakel. In July
and August, Faidherbe led a Franco-African force from Bakel to

Senudebu and into the formerly Bambuhu part of trans-Faleme
Bundu, to occupy the town of Kenieba, which Bundu ceded to
France. At that time, Bugul signed a treaty with Faidherbe on
behalf of all Bambuhu in which he granted the French full sov-
ereignty within any posts France might set up, and permitted
the French to build buildings, exploit mines, or cultivate the
land without payment.[23]

1859 Sambala of Xaaso attacked Farabana late in the year, claiming that slaves were escaping to Farabana and were not returned.
The siege of Farabana was lifted only in February or March of
1860. Toward the end of the year, or possibly January 1860,
Bugul died, and the succession passed to Banga with the agreement of Bugul's sons but contrary to the wishes of Mamadu Sili,
Bugul's nephew and a very powerful person.[24]

1858-60 The French tried to exploit the gold mines near Kenieba
under their own control (in territory ceded to them by Bundu
but previously claimed by Farabana as well). Low yields and
high mortality of the French staff forced them to abandon the
operations in 1860.

SOURCES

1. M. Delafosse, *Haut-Sénégal-Niger*, 3 vols. (Paris, 1912),
2:359-61.

2. Chambonneau to Marquis de Signalay, June 1688, ANS, C6 1.

3. Hodges to RAC, 16 September 1690, in Stone, "Journey of
Cornelius Hodges."

4. Bruë to Collé, 9 December 1716, BN, FF, NA, 9341.

5. Hodges to RAC, 16 September 1690, in Stone, "Journey of
Cornelius Hodges"; Saint-Robert to CI, 18 July 1725, ANF, C6 9;
Levens, 10 July 1725, FF, NA, 9339, ff. 141 ff.

6. Charpentier, Memorandum of 1 April 1725, ANF, C6 9; Levens
report 10 July 1725, FF, NA, 9339, ff. 141 ff.; Boucard, "Relation de Bambouc," June 1729, AM, 50/2, ff. 6-7.

7. Boucard, "Relation de Bambouc," ff. 6-7.

8. Le Regue to CI, 7 March 1731; CI to Claude Boucard, 12 May
1731; Pelays, Report of 1 June 1731, ANF, C6 10.

9. "Nouvel arrangement touchant la concession du Sénégal," BN,
FF, NA, 9341, ff. 33-98.

10. Hull, "Journey to Bundo," pp. 31, 34.

11. Extrait du Journal de M. David, BN, FF, NA, 4341, ff. 121-
23; unsigned annotation of Labat's *Relation* in ANF, C6 29. See
David, *Journal de voiage*, ed. Delcourt (in press).

12. Duliron, quoted in J. Machat, *Documents sur les établissements français et l'Afrique occidentale au xviie siècle* (Paris,
1906), pp. 52, 54.

13. Commandant Gajaaga to Conseil du Sénégal, 20 June 1754,
ANF, C6 14.

14. Aussenac to de la Bruë, Gajaaga, 22 May 1758, ANF, C6 14.
See also Machat, *Documents*, pp. 56 ff.

15. Major Houghton's report, Association for Promoting the
Discovery of the Interior Parts of Africa [the African Associa-
tion], *Proceedings*, 2nd ed., 2 vols (London, 1810), 1:247 ff.;

Durand, "Voyage du Sénégal à Galam par terre," ANF, C6 19, ff. 114-15; J. J. Lamartiny, *Etudes africaines: Le Bondou et le Bambouc* (Paris, 1884), pp. 55-56; Mammadi Madi Sy, CC, T 7 (2).

16. Major Houghton's report, African Association, *Proceedings*, 1:248.

17. Tourette, Report of 14 August 1829, ANS, 1 G 12; Duranton to Potin, 2 June 1824, and Duranton to Galam Company, 2 April 1824, ANS, 1 G 8; Grout de Beaufort to Roger, 8 June 1824, ANS, 1 G 7.

18. Detailed accounts of these events appear in the correspondence of F. Duranton with the Senegal government in ANS, 1 G 18.

19. D'Erneville to Governor, Senudebu, 27 November 1854, 13 G 166.

20. Flize to Governor, Bakel, 16 December 1855, and other despatches in ANS, 13 G 167.

21. Girardot to Governor, Senudebu, 22 March 1856, 13 G 167; L. Flize, "Exploration dans le Bambouk (Sénégal)," *Revue coloniale*, 17 (2nd ser.):384-89 (1857) and "Le Bondou (Sénégal)," *Revue coloniale*, 17 (2nd ser.):174-78 (1857).

22. L. Flize, "Le Bambouk," *Le Moniteur du Sénégal et dépendances*, 17 and 24 March, 1857, p. 3.

23. Cornu to Governor, 25 May 1858, *Moniteur du Sénégal*, 22 June 1858, pp. 2-3.

24. Pineau to Governor, Bakel, 24 December 1859 and 24 March 1860; Maritz to Governor, Keniéba, 14 February 1860, ANS, 13 G 168. For treaty texts see *Annuaire du Sénégal*, 1882, p. 94.

5 | CHRONOLOGICAL OUTLINES OF XAASO (KHASSO OR CASSON)

c. 1690's Amadu Awa Jaalo (Diallo) Aardo of the Fuulbe living
in the region of Kuniakari and Bafoulabé revolted against the
Malinke rulers and set up a separate kingdom, with the help of
charms furnished him by Eliman Maalik Sii of Bundu. Amadu Awa
himself was killed in the crucial and successful battle, and
the kingship passed to his son Seega Dua.[1] (See map 3.4.)

1698 Seega Dua was ruler of Xaaso.[2]

1725 Seega Dua was still ruler of Xaaso.[3]

1725-37 Within this interval, Jaje Gansiri, son of Seega Dua,
reigned.[4]

1737 Gimba Kinti, a second son of Seega Dua, reigned.[5]

1744 Compagnie des Indes established a factory at Kaiñu
(Caignou), by Felu Falls on the Senegal River. Demba Seega,
a third son of Seega Dua, reigned over some part of Xaaso.[6]

1751-58 This was a period of chronic warfare against Gajaaga
and against the Bambara of Kaarta.

1774 Awa Demba, son of Diba Sambala and ruler in the early nineteenth century, was born at about this time.[7]

1796? Demba Seega died after a long reign. In a war of succession that followed, Uri Jaje, son of Jaje Gansiri, opposed
Safere, son of Demba Seega's brother. Neither contestant won,
but a limited victory went instead to a third contender, Diba
Sambala, who entered and ruled briefly c. 1803-4. Upon his
death, the kingship passed to his brother, Muusa Xoi (c. 1804-
5), and was finally lost in a maze of claims and counter-claims,
with no clear victory to any contestant, though Awa Demba, who
was finally to win a kind of supremacy, was an active contestant after 1805.[8]

1819 The Bambara overran Xaaso, killed the unnamed ruling king,
and drove Awa Demba into refuge in the mountains of Bambuhu,
and then, for a period, to Bundu.[9]

c. 1822 Possibly earlier, the Galam Company reestablished a
French factory at Kaiñu.[10]

27

1824 In February and March, Awa Demba returned from Bundu and
attacked the forces of Seega Amadi, the village chief of
Tanke. With help from Bundu and Gidimaxa, Awa Demba was able
to establish himself at the village of "Maméry" in Logo,
though he was not strong enough to reconquer Xaaso proper,
north of the Senegal. Awa Demba's son, Kinta Sambala, had his
own establishment at Komantara, a little below Felu Falls.[11]

In May, Modiba of Kaarta invaded Logo with the largest army
that had recently been seen in Senegambia, but Awa Demba simultaneously crossed to the north bank and fortified himself in a
strong position. Checked in Logo, Modiba sent his cavalry on a
raid to support Farabana, his ally in Bambuhu. The raid did some
damage in Ñagala, another part of Bambuhu, but before the end of
June, Modiba recalled it, and the whole army retired to Kaarta.[12]

1827 Awa Demba permitted Duranton, acting as an agent of the
Senegalese government, to build a limited fortification at
Madina (Médine), near Felu Falls.

1829 In a major phase of the Xaaso civil war, Awa Demba's enemies
joined in an alliance under Safere, his uncle. The alliance began early in the year when Awa Demba was absent in Wuuli with
the greater part of his army, taking part in a long-distance
raid jointly with Bundu. Safere, whose base was in Tomoro,
north of the Senegal, planned a surprise attack, acting with
the ruler of Logo, the village chief of Dingira, the Baacili
ruler of Jakandape in Gajaaga, and the ruler of Ñagala in Bambuhu. But Awa Demba learned of this and struck first in May
by attacking Logo. F. Duranton aided, by using his artillery
to cover an assault on some Logankooɓe who had taken refuge on
an island in the Senegal. In August, Logo and its allies assembled for a major attack on Awa Demba's capital. On September
10, they sacked Madina and pillaged the French post, but they
failed to capture Awa Demba's own *tata* and were forced to with-
draw in the face of a counterattack. On December 16, the Logo-
Bambuhu allies again attacked Madina; but this time the defeat
turned into a rout, and they lost 600 dead, 400 prisoners, and
200 others captured and enslaved after the battle.[13]

1841 The French factory was withdrawn from Madina.[14]

1846 Awa Demba had by now died, the date of his death unknown.[15]

1849-51 War was carried on between Kinta Sambala, Awa Demba's
successor, and Malim Amadu, chief of Kulu.[16]

1851 Kinta Sambala continued as titular ruler of Xaaso, though
actually controlling no more than three villages in Logo.[17]

1853 Kaarta asked the Senegalese government to establish a fortified trading post at Madina, but the negotiations with Xaaso
and other problems held up construction until...

1854 when Juka Sambala (ruled 1854-80) succeeded Kinta Sambala,
and the old, indecisive war with Kulu continued.[18]

1855 In September, Senegal began actual construction of the new
fortified post at Madina.[19]

1857 From April 20 to July 18, Shaykh Umar besieged the Senegalese forces in Madina commanded by Paul Holle of Senegal, until
the fort was relieved by a Franco-Senegalese expedition sent
up river from Saint Louis.[20]

SOURCES

1. Oral traditions reported by J. Rémy, *La Sénégambie: Khasso* (n.p., n.d. [c. 1883]), pp. 8-9; F. V. Equilbecq, *Contes indigènes de l'ouest africain français*, 3 vols. (Paris, 1913-16), 1:271-74; L. J. B. Bérenger-Féraud, *Les peuplades de la Sénégambie: Histoire, ethnographie, moeurs, et coutumes, legendes, etc.* (Paris, 1879), pp. 215-18; C. Monteil, *Les Khassonké* (Paris, 1915), pp. 19-22.

2. Labat, *Nouvelle relation*, 3:290-93.

3. Charpentier, Memorandum of 1 April 1725, ANF, C6 9.

4. Monteil, *Khassonké*, pp. 21-24.

5. Saint-Adon, Report of 22 July 1737, ANF, C6 11. For oral traditions see Rémy, *Khasso*, pp. 10-11, and S. M. Cissoko, "Traits fondamentaux des sociétés du soudan occidental du xviie au début du xixe siècle," *BIFAN*, 31:1-30 (1969), p. 25.

6. Machat, *Documents*, pp. 46-55; David, *Journal de voiage* (in press).

7. Duranton to Galam Company, 2 April 1824, ANS, 1 G 8.

8. Monteil, *Khassonké*, pp. 29 ff.

9. Dupont to Governor, Bakel, 8 July 1819, ANS, 1 G 2.

10. Duranton to MC, 19 August 1828, ANS, 1 G 8.

11. Duranton to Galam Company, 2 April 1824, ANS, 1 G 8.

12. Duranton to Potin, Bakel, June 1824, ANS, 1 G 8.

13. Many despatches from Duranton to Governor and MC in ANS, 1 G 8.

14. Raffenel, Report of 14 March 1844, *Revue coloniale*, 4:172.

15. Zeler to Governor, 5 March 1836, ANS, 13 G 165.

16. Rey, "Rapport au gouverneur du Sénégal sur un voyage dans le Kasso, en juin et juillet 1851," *Revue coloniale*, 9 (2nd ser.): 241-75 (1852), p. 252.

17. Rey to Governor, 5 March 1851, ANS, 13 G 166.

18. Rey to Governor, 25 June 1853, 13 G 166; Monteil, *Khassonké*, p. 38; Rey to Governor, 10 April 1854, ANS, 13 G 166.

19. Cercle de Kayes, "Monographie," 1903-4, ANS, 1 G 310.

20. Principal report on this action by General Faidherbe is enclosed with Stephan to MC, no. 431, 10 August 1847, ANS, 2 B 32.

6 | CHRONOLOGICAL OUTLINES OF BUNDU

KING LIST

Traditions preserve many different king lists of Bundu, but the list collected by A. Rançon in the 1880's checks with the written record at so many points that it can be assumed to be approximately accurate. Where the written record suggests corrections, these are given in a separate column in the listing below. All of the rulers bore the surname or *yetooɗe* of Sii (Si), and were known collectively as the Sisiɓe.

	Rançon	Corrected
Maalik Dauda	1693-99[1]	
Bubu Maalik	1699-1718	(1700-1702)-(1719-27)[2]
Tumaane Bowi (Tumaane Bubu Maalik) (in other traditions, a four-year reign)	not mentioned	
Interregnum under Girobe domination	1718-28	ended between 1731 and 1735[3]
Maka Jiiba (Maka Bubu Maalik)	1728-64	(1731-35)-1764[4]
Amadi Gai	1764-85	1764-86[4]
Muusa Gai	1785-90	1786-90
Seega Gai	1790-94	1790-97[5]
Amadi Aisaata	1794-1819	1797-Jan. 1819
Muusa Yeero Maalik Aisaata	1819-27	1819-26[6]
Tumaane Moodi	1827-35	
Maalik Kuumba	1835-39	1835-37[7]
Saada Amadi Aisaata	1839-51	1837-51
Amadu Amadi Makumba	1852-53	
Interregnum and civil war	1852-54	
Umar Saane	1854-56[8]	
Bokar Saada	1856-85	
Umar Penda	1885-86	
Saada Amadi Saada	1886-88	
Usman Gaasi	1889-91	
Maalik Ture	1891-1905	

Notes to the King List

1. The earliest possible date for the foundation of Bundu would be 1690, since Cornelius Hodges passed through the territory in 1689 without mentioning it or Maalik Sii. Labat, *Nouvelle relation*, reports a traveler (allegedly in 1698) as saying that the rulers of the region inland from the Faleme bore the title of Eliman, the title Maalik Sii assumed and one which was not used elsewhere in the immediate region. This is in line with the reign lengths reported by Rançon and other collectors of oral tradition, and it is possible to count back from Maka Jiba, who met and talked to Thomas Hull when Hull visited Bundu in 1735. (Thomas Hull, "Voyage to Bundo" [1735], manuscript from the library of the Duke of Buccleuch.) The more precise date, 1693, is derived from a nineteenth-century traveler who reported the tradition that Bundu separated from Gajaaga 132 years before the date of his own visit. (Grout de Beaufort to Commandant Saint Louis, 20 January 1825, ANS, 1 G 7.) This is confirmed by another traditional account that 114 years elapsed between the foundation of Bundu and the death of Almaami Abdul Kader of Fuuta in A.H. 1221 (A.D. 1806-7), which yields the date A.D. 1692-93. (A. Kane, "Histoire et origine des familles du Fouta-Toro," CEHSAOF, 1:325-43 [1916], p. 341.) Similar elapsed-time data, however, can be found to give a variety of other dates from A.D. 1512 down to the late eighteenth century. These two are acceptable as evidence only because they are derived from independent sources, because they agree, and because they fall within limits that can be otherwise established. A. Rançon, "Le Bondou," *Bulletin de la Société de géographie de Bordeaux*, 17 (n.s.):433-63, 465-84, 497-584, 561-91, 593-647 (1894), remains the best general history and description of Bundu.

2. These estimated dates bracketing a period slightly later than Rançon's are derived from most generally accurate lists of reign lengths, using as a point of departure the fact that Maka Bubu Maalik was definitely in power in 1735. See P. D. Curtin, "Jihad in West Africa," *JAH*, 12:19-21 (1971).

3. The second date is from Hull's report in "Voyage to Bundo." The first is established by the fact that Maka Jiba had not returned from Fuuta before Yuuba Jaalo left for America in 1731. See P. D. Curtin, *Africa Remembered* (Madison, 1967), pp. 17-59.

4. French archival reports confirm that Maka Jiba was still Eliman in 1764, but the visit of Rubault to Bundu in 1786 found Amadi Gai still in office. (Durand, "Voyage du Sénégal à Galam par terre," ANF, C6 19, ff. 114-15.)

5. Mungo Park, who passed through Bundu in 1795, did not name the Almaami, but he did confirm the fact that the same Almaami had been in office at the time of Major Houghton's visit in 1791. That would stretch Seega's reign into early 1796 (M. Park, *Travels in the Interior Districts of Africa*, 2 vols. [London 1816-17], 1:78), and the further movement into 1797 is treated in D. Robinson, P. D. Curtin, and J. P. Johnson, "A Tentative Chronology of Fuuta Tooro from the Sixteenth through the Nineteenth Centuries," *CEA*, 12:555-92 (1972).

6. Muusa Yeero died in December 1826, and his successor was

selected early in 1827. (Duranton, Report of February 1826, ANS, 1 G 8; Renseignements laissé, July 1827, ANS, 13 G 164, 9.)

7. Saada's accession in 1837 is confirmed by William Fox, who visited Bundu early in 1838. (W. Fox, *A Brief History of the Wesleyan Missions on the Western Coast of Africa* [London, 1851], p. 477.)

8. The dates on either side of Umar Saane's reign are not generally accepted, since he was recognized by some factions and not by others. In the same sense, Bokar Saada's accession was a gradual conquest stretching over more than one year.

CHRONOLOGY OF EVENTS

1693 Foundation of Bundu by Maalik Sii.

1716 French report that Bundu was the most powerful state in the region of the upper Senegal.[1]

1724 Moroccan raids into Bundu through Gajaaga.[2]

1725 French post established at Kaiñura (near later Senudebu).[3]

1726 Chronic warfare between Bambuhu and Bundu on one side and the Baacili of Gajaaga on the other.[4]

1733 Further unfortified French factory established on the Faleme above Kaiñura.[5]

1735 Richard Hull traveled to Bundu and Bambuhu from the Gambia in the company of Yuuba Jaalo, a *juula* from Jamweeli in Bundu.[6]

1736-37 Hull's second trip to Bundu and Bambuhu.[7]

1737-38 Bundu and Xaaso joined Samba Gelaajo Jegi in a series of raids into Bambuhu, destroying the French fortified factories at Samarinacuta and Farabana.[8]

1740 Melchoir de Jaspas, an employee of the Royal African Company, visited Bundu and Bambuhu from the Gambia.[9]

1744 War between Bundu and Bambuhu.[10]

1751 The southern frontier of Bundu on the Faleme was 10 leagues south of Kidira, or measured in a direct line, near the present village of Tombura.[11]

1754 War between Bundu and Amadi Tumaane, ruler of Farabana in Bambuhu.[12]

1786 War between Bundu and Farabana.[13]

1791 Houghton reported that Bundu had won the war against Bambuhu and annexed part of the east bank of the Faleme, where the Almaami constructed a new capital.[14]

1797 Seega Gai was captured, tried, and executed at Marsa by Almaami Abdul Kader of Fuuta.[15] Civil War followed between the clerical party backing Amadi Paate and the secular party following Amadi Aisaata who won with the help of Gajaaga.

1801-2 An army from Bundu, Kaarta, and Xaaso first invaded Gajaaga, and then Fuuta, after having annexed part of lower Gajaaga to Bundu.[16]

1806-7 Amadi Aisaata invaded Fuuta, defeated and killed Abdul Kader at Guriki.[15]

1810 Bundu and Kaarta jointly attacked Wuli.[17]

1815-17 War between Kaarta on one side and Bundu and Xaaso on the other. Modiba of Kaarta marched into Bundu only to find

that the Bundunke army had left to attack Kaarta. As a result,
he captured all of Bulebane except the Almaami's own tata, but
the returning Bunduunke army caught the Bambara army in
scattered raiding parties and defeated it decisively (1817).

1818 War spread to an alliance of Fuuta and Bundu against upper
Gajaaga and Kaarta, with Safere of Xaaso also on the Kaarta
side. The Fuulbe were decisively defeated in early 1818 and
driven into Fuuta, but the Kaartan army withdrew from Bundu
with the coming of the rainy season, and the Fuulbe sued for
peace.[18]

1820-21 Bundu at first opposed and then agreed to the French
fortification of a post at Bakel. In the end, Bundu aided in
the French attack on Tiyaabu in 1821.[19]

1820's Chronic raids and counter-raids marked a period with
Bundu at war against lower Gajaaga, and with Bambara from
Kaarta raiding frequently into Bundu. Meanwhile Bunduunke
raids into Wuuli and other countries on the Gambia were made
almost every dry season.[20]

1832 May. Bundu and Wuuli were at war.[21]

1836 A Bambara-Xaaso cavalry force was allowed to pass through
Bundu in order to raid countries along the Gambia.[22]

1837 Bunduunke forces fought in Gajaaga on the side of Samba
Xumba Jaama, which brought Bambara raiders into Bundu again.[23]

1837-38 Almaami Saada extended his Gambia raids as far as
Saalum.[24]

1841 A Bunduunke-Kaartan army raided into upper Ñani on the
Gambia.[25]

1842 Alliance between Bundu and some of the chiefs of Xaaso attacked Tambukaane and Maxaana.[26]

1843 Almaami Saada signed a treaty with France for the construction of a fortified French factory at Senudebu.[27]

1845 Bundu was chronically at war with Gidimaxa.[28]

1846 A joint Fuuta-Bundu raid into Gidimaxa ended in failure
early in the year. Suraxe Fatima of Gucube formed an alliance
of Bundu, Goi, and Xaaso against Maxaana. The allies attacked
Maxaana in November, but failed to capture the town.[29]

1847 Bundu made peace with Maxaana and pulled out of its alliance with Suraxe, but it immediately entered Gambian affairs
on the side of Wuuli against Kantora and Karantaba. For his
expeditionary force to the Gambia, Almaami Saada drew on allies in Xaaso, in Bambuhu, and in Dentilia (February-March).
He made diplomatic contact with the English, which enabled him
to be tougher in his negotiation of outstanding conflicts with
the French over Senudebu.[30]

1848 April-May. Bundunke expedition against Wuuli.[31]

1849-50 Bundu declared war on Goi, but the only military action
took the form of Bundunke raids into Goi. (See chronicle of
Gajaaga, appendix 3.)

1853 Death of Almaami Amadu on September 17 led to civil war
between the supporters of Amadi Gai and Umar Saane, both of
the Bulebane branch of the Sisibe, but Amadi Gai had the support of the Kusan branch of the family.[32]

1854 September. Shaykh Umar appeared with his army at Farabana

in Bambuhu and called all factions to meet and make peace.
While there, Amadi Gai died (December), leaving Umar Saane as
the only contestant for the rulership, and Umar Saane joined
Shaykh Umar's jihad.

1855 Amadi Saada became the leader of those Sisibe who did not
follow Shaykh Umar, but that role passed to Bokar Saada by the
end of the year.[33]

1857 Bokar Saada, recognized as Almaami by France, conquered
Bundu and made his power effective with French aid. The crucial battle was the fall in August of Somsom tata to Faidherbe's
army returning from the relief of Madina in Xaaso.[34]

1858 A Franco-Bunduunke treaty of 18 August ceded certain commercial enclaves to France, but guaranteed Bunduunke independ-
ence on condition that Bundu not tax caravans making for the
French posts or stop emigration to French-held territory.[35]

Sources

1. Bruë to Collé, 9 December 1716, ANF, C6 5.
2. A. Delcourt, *La France et les etablissements français au
Sénégal entre 1713 et 1763* (Dakar, 1952), p. 163.
3. Unsigned memorandum dated 23 November 1725, ANF, C6 9.
4. Demoin, Memorandum of 7 April 1726, ANF, C6 9.
5. De Louard de Beaufort to CI, Gajaaga, 3 March 1733, ANF,
C6 10.
6. Hull, "Voyage to Bundo," passim.
7. RAC to Thomas Hull, 15 May 1735, T 70/55; Francis Moore to
African Committee, 29 April 1972, T 70/1518.
8. Conseil du Sénégal to CI, 15 February 1738, ANF, C6 11.
9. Gambia Accounts, 29 May 1740, T 70/573.
10. Conseil du Sénégal to CI, 28 July 1744, ANF, C6 12.
David, *Journal d'un voiage,* follows these events in
detail.
11. Conseil du Sénégal to CI, 20 August 1751, ANF, C6 10.
12. Commandant Galam to Conseil du Sénégal, 20 June 1754, ANF,
C6 14.
13. Durand, "Voyage à Galam," ff. 114-15.
14. African Association, *Proceedings,* 1:247, ff.
15. Robinson and others, "Chronology," p. xx.
16. Picard to MC, 20 June 1802, Laserre to MC, 16 February
1802, ANF, C6 21.
17. "Isaaco's Journal," Park, *Travels,* 2:240-42.
18. Gray, *Western Africa,* pp. 201-7.
19. Extensive correspondence from Bakel to Saint Louis in ANS,
1 G 2; Governor Sénégal to MC, 27 April 1821 and 12 July 1821,
ANS, 2 B 6. These events are also covered in some detail in
Marty, *Etudes sénégalaises,* pp. 166-71.
20. Commandant Bakel to Governor, 23 July 1824, ANS, 13 G
164; Chenaux, "Notes et renseignements," 26 August 1825, ANS,
13 G 164; Duranton, Report of February 1826, ANS, 1 G 8; Charles
Grant to R. W. Hay, 24 August 1829, CO 87/2.
21. Rendall to Hay, 4 June 1832, CO 87/6.
22. Commandant Bakel to Governor, 5 October 1836, ANS, 13
G 164.

23. Simon to Governor Sénégal, 25 October 1837, ANF-OM, Sénégal IV 15.

24. Fox, *Brief History*, pp. 455, 484.

25. Huntley to Lord John Russell, no. 73, 8 May 1841, CO 87/25.

26. Paul Holle to Governor Sénégal, 17 August and 29 August 1842, ANS, 13 G 164.

27. Raffenel, *Voyage dans l'Afrique*, pp. 340-41.

28. Paul Holle to Governor, Bakel, 24 October 1845, ANS, 33 G 164.

29. Extensive correspondence from Bakel to Governor in ANS, 13 G 165.

30. Correspondence from Senudebu to Saint Louis in ANS, 13 G 165 and 13 G 246; De Maricourt to MC, August 1847, ANS-OM, Sénégal IV 19; Raffenel, *Nouveau voyage*, 1:69-80.

31. Paul Holle to Commandant Bakel, 18 April 1848, ANS, 13 G 165.

32. Girardot to Governor, Senudebu, 21 September 1853, Paul Holle to Governor, Bakel, 1 July 1854, ANS, 13 G 166.

33. Extensive correspondence from Bakel and Senudebu to Governor, ANS, 13 G 166 and 13 G 167.

34. Commandant Bakel to Governor, 13 April 1857, ANS, 13 G 167; Stephan to MC, no. 456, 19 August 1845, Faidherbe to MC, no. 463, 29 August 1857, ANS, 2 B 32.

35. *Annuaire du Sénégal*, 1882, pp. 93-94.

7 | SAMPLE CENSUS AND POPULATION DATA

Population data for precolonial and early colonial Africa are notoriously bad. Estimates, even census data claiming to be based on actual count, are unreliable as well, but contemporaneous guesses are better than no data at all; especially when indications based on more reliable data from the early twentieth century are likely to be especially deceptive for the upper Senegal and Fuuta Tooro, which, authorities agree, underwent a very sharp drop in population beginning about the 1850's with the wars of Shaykh Umar. These contemporaneous estimates may therefore be useful indicators.

AFRICAN STATES

Wolof States

Waalo
   1675 Cavalry force, 6,000[1]
   1847 Total population, 16,000 (military strength, 2,500)[2]

Kajor
   1763 Dakar village population, 3,000[3]
   1764 Cavalry force, 1,000, infantry, 20,000[3]
   1810 Cavalry force, 5,000
         Cape Verde Republic, total population, 8,000[4]

Bawol
   1665 Rufisque town population, 1,600, including 3 resident French, 15 Portuguese men, and 1 Portuguese woman[1]
   1763 Rufisque town population, 3,000[3]
   1767 Lambai town population, 3,000[5]

36

Moorish States

Trarza
    1848   "Warrior tribes," 25,000 population, 6,000 fighting
            men
            "Maraboutic tribes," 30,000 population
            Total, 55,000[2]

Brakna
    1848   "Warrior tribes," 23,000 population, 5,000 fighting
            men
            "Maraboutic tribes," 40,000 population
            Total, 63,000[2]
    1859   Tichit town, 3,000 population, mainly Soninke[6]

Fuuta Tooro
c. 1752   Fighting force, 6,000-7,000[7]
    1848   Population, 1,000,000, fighting men, 30,000[8]
    1858   Population, 500,000[6]

Gajaaga
    1698   Dramane town population, 4,000[9]
    1700(?) Gunjuru town population, 4,000[10]
c. 1752   Fighting force 1,500-2,000, about half cavalry[7]
    1795   Jaxali town population, 2,000[11]
    1858   Total population of Gajaaga, 15,000-20,000[6]
            Arundu town population, 600[6]
            Bakel town, 2,495 population[6]
    1904   Population of Kamera or upper Gajaaga, 6,705[12]

Bundu
    1752   Military effectives, 7,000-8,000, half cavalry and
            half armed with firearms[7]
    1786   Kusan town population, 1,000-1,200[13]
    1838   Bulebane town population, 2,000[14]
    1843   Military effectives, 10,000 foot, 1,000 cavalry
            Bulebane town population, 2,000-2,500[15]
    1847   Bulebane town population, 2,800-3,000[16]
    1858   Total population, 100,000[6]
    1892   Total population, 10,000

Gidimaxa
    1904   Total population, 14,140[12]

Bambuhu
    1729   States of Samarina, Farabana, and Ñambia together
            could put 3,000 men into the field for military
            purposes[17]
c. 1752   Fighting force, 5,000-6,000, all infantry, one quarter
            armed with guns[7]
    1856   Farabana town population, 3,000[18]
    1858   Total population, 60,000[6]

Population of Bambuhu states	1887[19]	1904[12]
Nacaga (Natiaga)	---	2,334
Ñambia (Niambia)	1,900	---
Tambaura	2,510	2,120
Kamanä	1,000	1,428
Ñagala (Niagala)	4,360	5,587
Makana	1,112	299
Total in Cercle de Kayes		11,768

Dentilia
    1805 Juulafunda town population, 2,000[20]

Wuuli
c. 1500 Sutuko town population, 4,000[21]
    1847 Madina town population, 2,000[22]

ENGLISH ENCLAVES ON THE GAMBIA

1730 James Fort[23]

Chief officers, members of council	4
Factors	8
Writers	13
Skilled workers with English names, presumed to be English	17
Skilled workers with Purtuguese names, presumed to be Afro-Portuguese	4
Commander of the forces	1
Soldiers	35
Castle slaves	32
Total	114

(Represents normal complement if all posts were filled.)

1763 James Fort[24]

Civilian officials	3
European soldiers	8
Castle slaves	30
Dependents of castle slaves	13
Total	54

1826 Census of Bathurst[25]

	Male	Female	Total
White	28	2	30
Colored	64	58	122
Sailors (black and colored)	131		131
Blacks	791	786	1,577
Strangers, native traders	7		7
Total	1,021	846	1,867

1836 Census of MacCarthy's Island (Georgetown)[25]

	Male	Female	Total
White	7		7
Colored	777	375	1,152
Resident strangers	410		410
Total	1,194	375	1,569

1840 Census of Saint Mary's Island (Bathurst)[25]

	Male	Female	Total
White	38	4	42
Colored			3,221
Aliens			181
Total			3,444

1845 Census of Saint Mary's Island (Bathurst)[25]

	Male	Female	Total
White	43	7	50
Colored	1,860	1,786	3,646
Resident strangers	191		191
Total	2,094	1,793	3,887

SENEGAL AND DEPENDENCIES (SAINT LOUIS AND GORÉE)

1810 Under English occupation[26]

Slaves	5,466	
Free	3,202	Population 63 per cent slave
Total	8,668	

1832 Census[27]

	Male	Female	Total	Sex ratio per 1,000 females
Slaves	5,326	5,995	11,321	888
Free	1,331	1,639	2,970	882
Total	6,657	7,634	14,291	872
Per cent slave	80	79	79	

1844 Census[28]

	Muslim	Christian	Total
Europeans		235 (of whom 97 were women)	235
Free natives	5,726	1,795	7,521
Engagés à temps	798	3	801
Slaves	9,240	956	10,196
Total	15,764	2,989	18,753

Population was 4 percent engagé, 54 per cent slave, and 87 per cent Muslim.

SAINT LOUIS

1685 European population, 60[29]

1755 Population approximately 833 male, 1,667 female, 2,500 total[30]
Sex ratio per 1,000 females, 500
Partial occupational census of African male population:

   15 boat captains
   15 first mates
   36 sailors
    3 chief interpreters
   36 journeyman workers
   98 Company slaves
   550 slaves belonging to other residents
   753 total (86 per cent slave)

1758 Total population before British occupation, 2,923
      Total population after British occupation, 2,799[31]

1763 Total population, about 3,000[32]
      European staff of the Company of Merchants Trading to Africa:
            40 soldiers
            <u>12</u> civilians
            52 total

1765 Government servants of the Province of Senegambia[33]

	European	African	Total
Civilian officials	7		7
Craftsmen	5	6	11
Soldiers	33		33
Interpreters		3	3
Bakers		3	3
Laptots		81	81
Total	45	93	138

1776 Census of 24 January[34]

	Male	Female	Children	Total	Sex ratio per 1,000 females
Mulattoes	73	110		183	664
Free blacks	536	795		1,331	674
Slaves	1,077	1,770	261	3,108	608 (adults only)
Total	1,686	2,675	261	4,622	630 (adults only)
Per cent slave	64	66	100	67	

1779 Census[35]

	Male	Female	Children	Total
Habitants (free)	78	128		206
Wives and children of habitants		41	136	177
Slaves of habitants	478	979	401	1,858
Non-slave-owning free habitants	242	400	135	777
Total	798	1,548	672	3,018
Per cent slave	60	63	60	62

The population was 12 per cent Christian.
Sex ratio per 1,000 females was 562 for habitants, 605 for slaves

1785 Population estimates[36]

European (mainly soldiers)	700
Mulattoes	900
Free blacks	2,400
Slaves	2,000
Total	6,000
Per cent slave	33

1786 Population estimates[37]

Europeans, private	60
Europeans, government, including soldiers	600
Mulattoes and free Africans	2,400
Domestic slaves	2,400
Trade slaves in transit	1,000-1,200
Total, disregarding slaves in transit	5,460
Per cent slave, disregarding those in transit	44

1810   Population estimate[26]

	Free African	2,200
	Slaves	3,200
	Total	5,400
	Per cent slave	59

1832   Census[27]

	Male	Female	Total	Sex ratio per 1,000 females
Free	961	1,103	2,064	870
Slave	3,460	3,506	6,966	987
Total	4,421	4,609	9,030	
Per cent slave	78	76	77	

1838   Census of 1 January[38]

	Saint Louis proper	12,081
	Suburbs	1,636
	Total	13,717

GORÉE

1767   Census of 11 July[39]

	Male	Female	Total	Sex ratio per 1,000 females
Free	136	190	326	716
Slave	284	484	768	567
Total	420	674	1,094	
Per cent slave	68	72	70	

1776   Census of 18 April[40]

	Europeans	139
	Mulattoes	120
	Free blacks	110
	Slaves	1,200
	Total	1,569
	Per cent slave	76

1785   Census figure for number of proprietors, estimated numbers
   for other categories[37]

European soldiers and officials	70-80
Proprietors, including mulattoes and free Africans	116
Other free people	406
Domestic slaves	1,044
Trade slaves in transit	200
Total, disregarding slaves in transit	1,636-46
Per cent slave, disregarding those in transit	64

1810   Estimates[26]

	Europeans	10
	Mulattoes	502
	Free black	490
	Slaves	2,226
	Total	3,268
	Per cent slave	69

1832 Census[27]

	Male	Female	Total	Sex ratio per 1,000 females
Free	370	536	906	690
Slave	1,866	2,489	4,355	750
Total	2,236	3,025	5,261	739
Per cent slave	83	82	83	

STAFF OF THE COMPAGNIE DES INDES

1723 Staff levels planned by the Compagnie des Indes, by post in Senegambia[41]

	African	European	Total
Arguin	40	30	70
Saint Louis	50	60	110
Gorée	40	40	80
Albreda	5-6	5-6	10-12
Bissau		3-4	3-4
Fort Saint Joseph	15	15	30
Total	150-51	153-55	303-6

1734 European staff planned by the Compagnie des Indes, before and after staff cuts decided in 1734, by function[42]

	Before 1734	After 1734
Principals	49	38
Surgeons	9	6
Sailors	46	40
European domestics	8	3
European soldiers	76	26
Total	188	113

1720-36 European staff assigned to Gajaaga in selected years[43]

1720	16
1725	41
1734	44
1736	57

1629-1797 Size of the Garrison at Gorée under the Compagnie des Indes, the French, or the English Crown at various dates[44]

1692	35
1723	40
1725	25
1734	40
1736	39
1741	112
1755	40
1758	210
1763	126
1767	c. 200
1767-72	c. 160
1774-76	c. 100
1781	200 (English)
1784 (March)	30

1784 (April)	50
1789	30-40
1797	10

1736 European and African staff in the service of the Company as of 1 May 1736[43]

	Saint Louis	Gorée and Gambia	Gajaaga	Total
European				
Managing council	5	3	3	11
Clerks	17	9	6	32
Craftsmen	26	12	4	42
Sailors	43	8	3	54
Soldiers	17	35	20	72
Domestics	1	--	--	1
Subtotal (European)	109	67	36	212
African				
Sailors (not counting seasonal employees)	16	30	26	72
Craftsmen	21	6	11	38
Cooks and gardeners	11	6	5	22
Castle slaves used as sailors	94	--	--	94
Others	--	8	--	8
Subtotal (African)	142	50	42	234
Grand Total	251	117	78	446

SOURCES

1. Ritchie, "Deux textes," p. 310n.
2. Caille, "Notes sur les peuples de la Mauritanie et de la Nigritie, riverains du Sénégal," *Revue coloniale*, 10:1-10 (1846).
3. Doumet, "Mémoire historique sur Gorée," ANF, C6 29.
4. Maxwell, Replies to H. M. Commissioners, 1 January 1811, CO 267/29.
5. ANF, C6 15.
6. G. Lejean, "Le Sénégal en 1859 et les routes commerciales du Sahara," *Revue contemporaine*, 11:368-403 (1859), p. 388.
7. "Mémoire sur les mines de Bambouc," BN, FF, NA, 9557, f. 165.
8. E. Bouët-Willaumez, *Commerce et la traite des noirs aux côtes occidentales d'Afrique* (Paris, 1848), p. 32 ff.
9. Labat, *Nouvelle relation*, 3:333.
10. La Courbe, in *Premier voyage*, ed. Cultru, p. vi.
11. Park, *Travels*, 1:96-97.
12. Monographie du Cercle de Kayes, 1903-4, ANS, 1 G 310.
13. J. B. L. Durand, *Voyage au Senegal*, 2d ed. in 2 vols. (Paris, 1807), 2:22. First published, Paris, An X (Sept. 1802-Sept. 1803).
14. Fox, *Brief History*, p. 473.

15. Raffenel, *Voyage dans l'Afrique*, p. 134.
16. Raffenel, *Nouveau voyage*, 1:52.
17. E. Roux, *Notice historique sur le Boundou* (Saint Louis, 1893); also found in mss. in ANS, 1 G 78.
18. Flize, "Le Bambouk," p. 387.
19. Vallière, "Notice sur le Bambuk," 1884, ANS, 1 G 85.
20. Park, *Travels*, 2:57-59.
21. J. Boulègue, "La Sénégambie du milieu du xve siècle au début du xviie siècle" (Ph.D diss., 3rd cycle, University of Paris, 1969), p. 67.
22. Ingram, "Abridged Account of an Expedition of about Two Hundred Miles up the Gambia, *JRGS*, 17:150-155 (1847), p. 154.
23. F. Moore, *Travels into the Inland Parts of Africa . . .* (1738), pp. 14-15.
24. Return of 10 November 1763, CO 388/52, f. 61.
25. Gambia Blue Book for 1850, CO 90/24.
26. Maxwell, replies to H.M. Commissioners, 1 January 1811, CO 267/29.
27. *Statistiques coloniales*, 1832.
28. Thomas, Passation de service, 11 December 1845, ANS, 13 G 22.
29. La Courbe, *Premier voyage*, p. 39.
30. Conseil du Sénégal, réponse au mémoire de Sieur Godheu [of February 1754], undated, ANF, C6 14.
31. Duranger, "Journal," 2 July 1758, ANF, C6 14.
32. J. Barnes to African Committee, 9 July 1764, CO 388/52.
33. Return of 16 March 1765, CO 388/52.
34. CO 267/1. The original adds up to the incorrect total of 4,736.
35. ANS, 22 G 1.
36. Estimated by Durand in *Sénégal*, 2:26, and by Saugnier in *Voyages*, p. 178, modified by additional data from Jore, "Etablissements français," p. 260.
37. S. M. X. de Golberry, *Fragmens d'un voyage en Afrique, fait pendant les années 1785, 1786, 1787, dans les contrées occidentales de ce continent . . .*, 2 vols. (Paris, An X [1802]), 1:154, 2:60.
38. *Moniteur du Sénégal*, no. 95, 5 January 1858, p. 1.
39. ANF, C6 17. M. H. Knight-Baylac, "La vie à Gorée de 1677 à 1789," *RHCF*, 58:377-420 (1970), p. 402, produced a table of Gorée non-European populations from 1749 to 1786 covering a greater variety of Sources than are used here and below, many of the data taken from an unpublished manuscript by a Dr. Cariou, "Promenade à Gorée," which is presumably available in Dakar but which I have not seen.
40. ANF, C6 15.
41. "Mémoire sur le commerce du Sénégal, 11 October 1723, ANF, C6 7.
42. Règlements du Sénégal, 8 October 1734, ANF, C6 11.
43. Delcourt, *La France au Sénégal*, pp. 114-17, 400-404.
44. Compiled from a variety of sources by Knight-Baylac in "La vie à Gorée," p. 388.

8 | SLAVE PRICES IN SENEGAMBIA

Slave prices are a problem of some difficulty, yet crucial to the development of the tropical Atlantic economies. Two special features of the Senegambian slave trade tend to interfere with accurate reporting of prices. One is the inaccuracy of reporting a bar price multiplied by a conventional value of the bar in some European currency. (See chapter 6.) The value of a bar varied with each commodity, and the actual prices paid (measured by some standard such as the English value of the goods exchanged for the slave) can only be determined with accuracy in those periods when the surviving record is rich enough to show a large number of transactions in a single year, or else to establish an average general exchange rate between the bar and a European currency for the whole range of commodities traded in that year. In fact, this has been attempted here only for the years 1683-88 and again for 1727-41, when actual transactions are recorded on the books of the Royal African Company and these books have survived. (T 70/546 and T 70/576.) For other years, one or more prices may be reported, but usually as a statement by a contemporaneous observer that the "ordinary price" of slaves was so much. These statements sometimes differ from one another, and the simple solution of putting them all on a graph and running a line midway between them is no solution at all. The deviant reports that can be examined in detail usually turn out to be special situations, not random variation.

The principal cause of deviant price reports was the point of sale. Few prices were quoted f.o.b. James Island or f.o.b. Gorée. The Royal African Company's accounts, for example, show the price the Company paid to its African supplier. These prices varied according to the seller, the source of the slaves, the quantity of the sale (since bulked slaves ready for shipment were always more valuable than those that came in a few at a time and had to be held till a full cargo was ready), and the place of the sale. The Royal African Company, like the Afro-French traders

45

on the Senegal, was in fact a carrier over routes as long as 300 kms within Africa, and it performed a complex variety of bulking, brokerage, and storage functions before it had a saleable cargo to offer by the waterside. The price the Company paid for the slaves it bought was only part of its total outlay for a cargo of slaves f.o.b. James Island. The only useful indication of the f.o.b. price is therefore the price the Company charged to "separate traders." The equivalent for the Compagnie des Indes would be the price paid for the slaves, plus a pro rata addition for the cost of maintaining the forts, garrisons, and factories.

But the situation is still more complicated because the distribution of functions between ships and forts was not constant. After 1779 on the Gambia, the Company was out of business, replaced by a variety of shoreside merchants scattered along the river. In the usual pattern of trade, a ship sailed upriver, traded here and there until it had a cargo, and then sailed directly to the Americas. This meant that some of the brokerage and much of the cost of river transportation once included as part of a price f.o.b. James Island now had to be borne by the ocean shipper. In effect, it was no longer possible to buy a cargo of slaves f.o.b. James Island. Exact comparison is therefore impossible, just as it is between the cost of "one automobile" in 1910 and 1950.

The raw prices are nevertheless reported in table A8.1—not as a valid and continuous price series but as a store of data that might be useful to other researchers interested in comparative prices.

The next problem is to translate the raw prices of table A8.1 into time series of comparable prices for the Gambia and Senegal respectively. This cannot be done in a completely satisfactory way, but markups between interior points and the coast can be taken into account to produce a continuous series that, for all its weakness, is better than the raw data of table A8.1. For the Gambia, the usual markup of the Royal African Company for bulking, brokerage, and storage can be deduced from the Company's accounts of the 1730's. The markup of the samples for 1732 and 1736 is the least equivocal, a mean of 61 per cent. (Other transactions are recorded, but the terms of sale are subject to possible misunderstanding. The sample for 1730 is also set aside, since the RAC officials in London called the Gambia staff to account for selling those slaves at an unprofitable price.) As ships began sailing further upriver and taking on more of the bulking functions on their own, the markup would be expected to drop. A comparison of the mean prices paid upriver in 1750 and 1752, against the f.o.b. price reported for Albreda in 1752, indicates a markup of 33.4 per cent, and this coefficient is used for adjusting Gambia prices from 1750 onward.

For the French trade on the Senegal, the large sample of 1737-40 is part of a calculation made at the time for the Compagnie des Indes, including the cost of maintaining the forts. It indicated that the Compagnie des Indes had a mean markup of 76.2 per cent between the price it paid for slaves and the actual cost at the point of ocean shipment. This calculation included some long-distance trade from Gajaaga as well as strictly local trade at Gorée or in Waalo, but it is nevertheless used for translating the cost of slaves reported for Saint Louis into the f.o.b. cost. Where Gorée prices are concerned, the sample of 1772 indicates a markup of 33 per cent from purchase on the *petite côte* to sale f.o.b. Gorée, and this is used for the Gorée trade. The prices reported for the Gajaaga trade for 1786 are also taken as a general indication of the order of markup necessary to bring slaves down from the interior for sale f.o.b. Saint Louis, and the markup was 293 per cent.

Even though these coefficients are no more than rough estimates, when applied to the raw prices of table A8.1, they yield the time series shown in table A8.2. Whatever their demerits, the two price series now show a regular and simultaneous movement of the prices at the two river mouths, even though they are based on independent bodies of data. (See figure 4.1.)

Table A8.2 gives the prices in sterling equivalents, which, over such long periods, might not mean very much in real terms. Rough calculations of changing import values, however, indicate virtually constant import values for the 1730's compared with the 1680's. For the interval from the 1730's to the 1780's, import prices inflated by about one third, then deflated again over the next half-century to the 1830's. If these changes are applied in sequence to the whole 150-year period, the net change is a decline in import prices of about 18 per cent. (See table 4.1 and chapter 8.) Within the range of accuracy possible with the available data, the prices in table A8.2 can be taken as nearly equivalent to real prices, though modification at half-century intervals should be slightly more accurate.

Table A8.1
Slave Prices in Senegambia at Varying Points
and with Varying Conditions of Sale, 1664-1855

Symbols:
  A A calculation based on the amounts and invoice values of the goods enter-
     ing into a recorded transaction or series of transactions
  B A calculation made by a contemporaneous official or merchant from the
     account books of a firm actually in the trade
  C A contemporaneous report of an actual transaction, but without precise
     reference to the prime cost of the goods involved
  D A contemporaneous report of the "usual price" or "ordinary price"
  E Retrospective report of what price was "ordinary" in the past

All franc or livre prices translated to sterling at the rate indicated
in appendix 9.

Date	No. of slaves	Prices paid to African slave merchants				Prices f.o.b.	
		Lower Gambia	Gorée	Lower Senegal	Gajaaga	St. Louis	James Ft., vicinity
1664	1	£3.61 A[1]					
1676-88		3.00 E[2]					
1682				£4.61 D[3]			
1683	33	3.61 A[4]					
1684	163	3.81 A[4]					
1685	270	2.96 A[4]		4.64 D[5]			
1686	461	3.30 A[4]					
1687	238	3.52 A[4]					
1688	363	3.18 A[4]					
1693		2.69 D[6]		2.24 D[6]			
1698- 1707		8-21 E[2]					
1698					£1.65 D[6]		
1699	1	3.85 A[7]					
1700				3.85 D[6]			
1704	32	2.55 A[8]					
1717					2.97 E[9]		
1718					3.65 D[9]		
1723		7.12 D[9]	£5.34	3.65	2.27 D[9]		
1724				1.54[10]			
1727	18	5.57 A[11]					
1728	25	6.41 A[11]					
1729	15	5.01 A[11]					
1730	84	7.19 A[11]					£ 8.33 B[12]
1731	65	3.92 A[11]					
1732	96	5.38 A[11]					10.00 A[13]
1733	8	3.54 A[11]					
1734	19	4.54 A[11]					
1735	67	5.41 A[11]					
1732-40	8,773					£14.34[14]	
1736	225	7.34 A[11]					10.00 A[15]
1737	26	7.71 A[11]					
1738	5	5.94 A[11]					
1739	93	5.07 A[11]					9.00 A[16]
1737-40				9.07 B[17]		15.98 B[17]	
1738-40						14.95 B[18]	
1740	160	7.52 A[11]					
1741	37	5.51 A[11]					
1745		7.96 D[19]					

(continued)

Table A8.1 (continued)

Date	No. of slaves	Prices paid to African slave merchants				Prices f.o.b.	
		Lower Gambia	Gorée	Lower Senegal	Gajaaga	St. Louis	James Ft., vicinity
1750		£ 6.34 D[20]					
1752							£14.40 D[21]
1754		6.00 D[22]					12.00 D[22]
1755							12.00 D[23]
1758							12.80 E[24]
1761							14.50 D[25]
1764				£11.81 D[26]			
1765	60			8.96 A[27]			
1770		10.27 D[28]					
1772			£11.85 D[29]			£15.80 D[29]	
1773						21.00 B[30]	
1776			12.71 D[31]				
1782		9.57 D[32·]					
1783				13.92 D[33]			
1784		21.84 D[34]					
1785						£ 6.86 B[35]	29.75 D[35]
1786						9.39 B[36]	27.52 B[36]
1795		19.00 D[37]					
1809			19.80 D[38]				
1814						8.00 D[39]	
1822						7.76 D[40]	
1825-29						9.11 B[41]	
1826						9.26 D[42]	
1827						14.77 D[43]	
1828						13.69 D[41]	
1830						12.54 D[44]	
1832						11.76 D[45]	
1838				19.40[46]			
1847			13.27[47]	16.10[47]			
1848						7.38 D[48]	
1852						11.85 D[49]	
1855						7.61 D[50]	

Sources:
1. Gambia Journals, 4 March 1664, T 70/544.
2. Board of Trade Report, looking back from 1788.
3. J. J. Le Maire, *Voyage to the Canaries, Cape Verd, and the Coast of Africa under the Command of M. Dancourt* (Edinburgh, 1887), p. 35. Translated by Edmund Goldschmid from the French edition of 1695. Price quoted in French currency.
4. Calculated from Gambia Journals, T 70/546. The actual prices paid for slaves were recorded in bars at this period, but invoices indicate the prime cost in England of the goods imported during each of these years, which makes it possible to calculate an average £/bar ratio, which can then be multiplied by the average bar price paid for slaves. (See chapter 6.)
5. La Courbe, *Premier voyage*, p. 96. Price quoted in French currency.
6. Labat, *Nouvelle relation*, 3:338, 4:319. Prices quoted in French currency.
7. Gambia Journals, T70/547, 21 February 1698/99.
8. Gambia Journals, T 70/834, 24, 26, and 28 April, and 1 and 3 May, 1704.
9. Prices for 1718 and 1719 in bars from Brüe to Violaine, 23 October 1719, ANF, C4 5; 1723 from "Mémoire sur le commerce du Sénégal," 11 October 1723, ANF, C6 7. Because of rapid fluctuations in French currency in this period, the 1717 and 1718 prices are based on the change of bar values between those dates and 1723, when the bar-Saint Louis was thought to be worth 6 livres and the bar-Galam

(continued)

Table A8.1 sources (continued)

worth 4. But the raw data yields £2.27 for Saint Louis and £3.65 for Gajaaga.
It is assumed that these were reversed.

10. Price quoted is that of Escale du Désert, and hence lower than that at
Saint Louis itself. J. Demoin, "Extrait de la traite de gomme . . ." 10 August
1724, ANF, C6 8.

11. Calculated from Gambia Journals, T 70/550 through 575, by collecting sample
transactions from the first half of each year and multiplying the quantity of
each commodity exchanged by the invoice prices of goods shipped from England.
The numbers of sales in any one year are sometimes inadequate from a statistical point of view, but the sample should be adequate for periods of five years
or more.

12. The transaction was in bars—65 bars per slave, taken to be worth £.128
per bar (the average £/bar ratio for the years 1729-31). The Company thought
that this price was too low to be profitable. RAC to Anthony Rogers et al., 30
July 1730, T 70/35.

13. Gambia Journals, T 70/559, 16 February 1732/33.

14. "Sénégal 1731 à 1740," ANF, C6 12, purporting to be a report of the Compagnie des Indes' actual operations. Their loss at sea in this period was 7 per
cent of the slaves shipped. With a net cost in Africa, including the cost of
operating the shore establishments, of 360 livres (£14.34), the total cost of
shipping came to an average of 171 livres (£6.81) per slave landed alive in the
Americas. The average selling price was 774 livres (£30.81), leaving a gross
profit of £9.67 per slave landed. Even so, the writer pointed out that this
profit assumed speedy and complete payment by the planters, where in fact slaves
were sold on credit and some of these advances would never be recovered. The
gross profit therefore included a substantial premium for risk.

15. Gambia Journals, T 70/565, 8 May 1736.

16. Gambia Journals, T 70/571, 5 May 1739.

17. "Mémoire sur la prix des noirs," ANF, C6 8, based on the costs of trade
goods exchanged for the slaves through three trade years from 1737-38 to 1739-
40. Purchase price is an average, regardless of point of purchase.

18. A calculation, apparently without the full Company account books available, but based on total costs including those of the shore establishment, with
allowance for the nonslave returns direct to France but neglecting the government subsidies which had the effect of reducing the Company's f.o.b. cost
in Saint Louis. "Etat de la dépense de la concession du 1ère juin 1738 au
31 mai 1740," ANF, C6 12.

19. "Commerce de la concession du Sénégal," ANF, C6 12.

20. Undated memorandum in ANF, C6 29.

21. Conseil du Sénégal to CI, 21 October 1752, ANF, C6 13.

22. Conseil du Sénégal to CI, 20 August 1754, ANF, C6 14.

23. Skinner to Africa Committee, 28 April 1755, T 70/30, listed as f.o.b. in
the upper river.

24. Memorandum of 2 November 1762, ANF, C6 14.

25. Debat to Africa Committee, James Fort, 20 August 1761, T 70/30.

26. Doumet, "Mémoire sur Gorée . . ." ANF, C6 29.

27. "Assortment of Goods for about 60 Bambara Negroes," CO 388/52.

28. Beudet, Memorandum of 30 October 1770, ANF, C6 16.

29. Memorandum of 26 December 1772, ANF, C6 16. Price listed under Gorée is
actually the price on the petite côte, while the price listed under f.o.b. Saint
Louis is valid as f.o.b. Gorée.

30. Rastel de Rocheblave to Boniface, 1773, "Observations sur Gorée, ANF, C6
16. The price in this case is the actual price paid by the French commandant
on Gorée to the British Governor in Fort Lewis for slaves sent down from the
Senegal to Gorée.

31. Bellecombe and Chavreau to MC, 19 April 1776, ANF, C6 17.

32. Unsigned despatch no. 67, ANF-OM, DFC Sénégal 2.

33. Raybaud, "Administration du Sénégal," p. 160.

34. A standard price at which slaves were carried on the accounts, "Etat des
captifs, etc. traité au mois de décembre 1784," ANF, C6 18.

35. Saugnier, Voyages, pp. 316-19. The Gajaaga price is given as an example
of the low cost of French goods in exchange for slaves, if the assortment is

(continued)

Table A8.1 sources (continued)

carefully made. It should therefore be treated as a minimal estimate.

36. A near-contemporary with some knowledge of Senegambia, preparing a plan for colonization in 1802, took Saugnier's data, which he recognized as extreme, and calculated these prices for 1786. He chose the lower end of Saugnier's range for Saint Louis prices, and he added the cost of tolls to the minimum cost of slaves in Gajaaga. Where Saugnier indicated a 333 per cent markup between buying price in Gajaaga and selling price in Saint Louis, this authority's modified data yield a markup of only 293 per cent, which is accepted as preferable because more clearly in line with other data. ("Un plan de colonisation de Sénégal en 1802," *CEHSAOF*, 1:130-214 (1916), 1:136, 182, 184.)

37. Park, *Travels*, 1:37.

38. Maxwell to Secretary of State, 15 January 1809, CO 267/32.

39. Picard, Plan of 22 Sept. 1814, ANF-OM, Sénégal XIII 17. The price in this case is only his estimate.

40. Governor Senegal to MC, 11 November 1822, ANS, 2 B 7. A year earlier, Major Gray reported a price of £7.40 in Kaarta (Gray, *Western Africa*, p. 347).

41. Zuccerelli, "Engagés à temps," p. 432.

42. Enclosure with Governor Senegal to MC, 16 December 1826, ANF-OM, Sénégal XIII 7.

43. Faure, "La garnison européene du Sénégal (1779-1858)," *RHCF*, 8:5-108 (1920), p. 38. This was the actual average price paid for 17 military slaves in Bakel.

44. Faure, "Garnison européene," pp. 56-58.

45. Rendale to Hay, no. 42, 3 August 1831, CO 87/5.

46. Guillet, "Notes de l'ordonnateur," 29 January 1836, ANS, K7. The price in this case is proposed compensation for manumission of a slave.

47. R. Pasquier, "A propos de l'émancipation des esclaves au Sénégal en 1848," *RHCF*, 54:188-208 (1968). Figure is a proposed judicial compensation. But the *Bulletin administratif*, 4:30-31, 35, listing several compensations, suggests a mean price of £34.92, which probably represents the assessed value of a domestic slave, not an untrained new slave.

48. Holle to Reverdit, 10 June 1848, ANS, 13 G 165.

49. Rey to Governor Senegal, 12 March 1872, ANS, 13 G 176.

50. Parent to Governor Senegal, 10 November 1855, ANS, 13 G 167.

Table A8.2
Slave Prices in Senegambia, Adjusted to Values
f.o.b. Coastal Ports, 1664-1855

* Signifies price reported in the sources (from table A8.1); prices otherwise calculated as explained in text above.

Date	St. Louis or Gorée	James Ft. or vicinity
1664	---	£ 5.81
1682	£ 8.12	---
1683	---	5.81
1684	---	6.13
1685	8.18	4.77
1686	---	5.31
1687	---	5.67
1688	---	5.12
Mean 1681-90	£8.15	£5.47
1693	3.95	4.33
1698	4.84	---
1699	---	6.20
1700	6.78	---
Mean 1691-1700	5.19	5.27
1704	---	4.11
1717	8.71	---

(continued)

Table A8.2 (continued)

Date	St. Louis or Gorée		James Ft. or vicinity	
1718	£10.70		---	
Mean 1711-20		£ 9.71		---
1723	6.72		£11.46	
1724	4.51		---	
1727	---		8.97	
1728	---		10.32	
1729	---		8.07	
1730	---		8.33*	
Mean 1721-30		5.61		£ 9.43
1731	---		6.31	
1732	---		10.00*	
1733	---		5.70	
1734	---		7.31	
1735	---		8.71	
1736	---		10.00*	
1737	---		12.41	
1738	---		9.56	
1739	---		8.16	
1740	---		12.11	
Mean 1731-40		14.38*[1]		9.03
1741	---		8.87	
1745	---		12.82	
1750	---		8.46	
Mean 1741-50		---		10.05
1752	---		14.40*	
1754	---		12.00*	
1755	---		12.00*	
1758	---		12.80*	
Mean 1751-60		---		12.80
1761	---		14.50*	
1764	20.81		---	
1765	15.72		---	
1770	---		13.70	
Mean 1761-70		18.27		14.10
1772	15.80*		---	
1773	21.00*		---	
1776	16.90		---	
Mean 1771-80		17.90		---
1782	---		12.77	
1783	24.53		---	
1784	---		29.13	
1785	29.75		---	
Mean 1781-90		27.14		20.95
1795	---		25.35	
Mean 1791-1800		27.52*[2]		---
1809	26.33		---	
1814	23.45		---	
1822	22.75		---	
1825	26.70[3]		---	
1826	27.14		---	
1827·	43.29		---	
1828	40.13		---	
1830	36.75		---	
Mean 1821-30		32.79		---
1832	34.47		---	
1836	34.18		---	
Mean 1831-40		34.33		---

(continued)

Table A8.2 (continued

Date	St. Louis or Gorée		James Ft. or vicinity
1847	£23.01		---
1848	21.63		---
Mean 1841-50		£22.32	---
1852	34.73		---
1855	22.31		---
Mean 1851-60		28.52	---

Sources:

1. Price reported is the calculated cost to the Compagnie des Indes, including the cost of maintaining the shore stations for the period 1732-40, or the average cost per unit for 8,773 slaves.

2. A calculation applying to the whole period 1784-99. The observations for the 1780's are so close to this figure that it is taken as valid for the 1790's alone.

3. Reported as the price paid for slave-soldiers (adjusted to Saint Louis values) for the years 1825-29, but used here as the price of a single year, since the prices rose sharply in 1827. (Zuccarelli, "Engagés à temps," p. 432.)

9 | CONVERSION OF EUROPEAN MONETARY VALUES

The study of the Senegambian economy poses special problems because of the implication of two European trading nations each of which preserved records in its own currency. The value of two different currencies is difficult to measure. They may be exchanged for each other in different markets at approximately equal values, but the market value may not represent the direct equivalent that either will bear to silver or gold. In addition, the market value will not necessarily represent the purchasing power of the money at a particular place or time. That is, it could often happen that someone living an ordinary middle class life in Paris could buy 20 per cent more with pounds sterling exchanged for livres than he could buy if he had been spending sterling for the same purchases in London, or vice versa. The point in this instance is that eighteenth-century price schedules differed between European countries even more than they do today. This meant that no set rate of exchange could possibly represent the exact equivalent purchasing power of one currency in another currency—it all depended on what the money was to be spent for.

It is nevertheless important to seek some kind of approximate equivalence. Many economic historians have tried to turn all values into an equivalent quantity of silver, or into an equivalent number of hours of ordinary labor in that market. Either of these methods is adequate for certain purposes, but the labor-cost system is not appropriate for dealing with a non-Western economy with differing labor costs. The advantages of the silver equivalent system can be had in part by using the pound sterling as the basic currency, simply because sterling remained defined as equal to 27.8397 grams of pure silver from 1671 to 1797. In 1797, Britain went to a bimetallic system until 1816, and then to a gold standard, but silver coins remained at 26.1524 grams of pure silver per pound until 1914. The bimetallic problems that followed were not to be severe until after 1850, and the revaluation

in terms of silver in 1816 was small, given the tolerances possible in a study like this one. The pound sterling between 1670
and 1850 can therefore serve as a constant equivalent to a fixed
silver standard. The silver content of the livre tournois fluc-
tuated more widely, especially in the late seventeenth and early
eighteenth century. Most Senegambian values have therefore been
expressed in pounds sterling.

Where possible, market prices of foreign exchange were preferred
to par values based on the metallic content of the coins. Some
market prices are available from the Amsterdam exchange, where
quotations for the Dutch schellingen were given in both livres
tournois and pounds sterling; others are London prices. When
several quotations were given for a single year, the mean of the
quotations is taken as the annual price. Years with missing
data are filled in by interpolation as indicated. In some instances, especially when the par value altered during the course
of the year, par values were used instead of market prices. The
changing definitions of the livre and the pound sterling in terms
of pure silver are taken from D. L. Wiedner, "Coins and Accounts
in West European and Colonial History, 1250-1936" (Ph.D. diss.,
Harvard University, 1958), pp. 223-33, 342-44. In most years
of changing definitions, the annual value was based on par values
weighted according to the duration of each. In some years, like
1720, par values changed so often that the median between high
and low values for the year was adopted instead.

The period of the French Revolution is particularly difficult.
Exchange rates after 1790 were regularly published in the British
Parliamentary Papers, but they depart so far from par values in
some of the war years between 1791 and 1815 that the par values
are preferred until 1816. Where bimetallism presents alternate
par values in these years, the gold values are preferred. From
1816 onward, the annual values are the mean of the first quotation for each month.

The following annual quotations of livre-sterling or livre-
franc equivalents were established for purposes of this study.
Any superscript applies to the quotation for the indicated year
and all following years until a new superscript is encountered.

Value of One Livre Tournois or One Franc in Decimal Pounds Sterling

1671	.0770[1]	1686	.0748	1701	.0629	1716	.0502
1672	.0761	1687	.0744	1702	.0595[3]	1717	.0502
1673	.0779[2]	1688	.0733	1703	.0613[1]	1718	.0512[1]
1674	.0796	1689	.0735[2]	1704	.0629[3]	1719	.0352[5]
1675	.0791	1690	.0751	1705	.0574	1720	.0383[2]
1676	.0770	1691	.0728[1]	1706	.0582[1]	1721	.0413[5]
1677	.0761	1692	.0726	1707	.0631[4]	1722	.0424
1678	.0742	1693	.0746	1708	.0664[1]	1723	.0445
1679	.0752	1694	.0788	1709	.0673	1724	.0340
1680	.0775	1695	.0836	1710	.0663	1725	.0307[2]
1681	.0765	1696	.0857	1711	.0496[3]	1726	.0274[5]
1682	.0768	1697	.0840[2]	1712	.0496	1727	.0305
1683	.0754	1698	.0823	1713	.0497	1728	.0305
1684	.0764[2]	1699	.0807[1]	1714	.0580[1]	1729	.0306
1685	.0773[1]	1700	.0654	1715	.0661[3]	1730	.0308

(continued)

Value of One Livre Tournois or One Franc in Decimal Pounds Sterling (continued)

Year	Value	Year	Value	Year	Value	Year	Value
1731	.0316	1761	.0320	1791	.0421	1821	.0384
1732	.0310	1762	.0325	1792	.0398[3]	1822	.0388
1733	.0316	1763	.0315	1793	.0398	1823	.0384
1734	.0320	1764	.0328	1794	.0398	1824	.0389
1735	.0318	1765	.0323	1795	.0398	1825	.0382
1736	.0320	1766	.0315	1796	.0400	1826	.0386
1737	.0398[3]	1767	.0316	1797	.0403	1827	.0389
1738	.0398	1768	.0317	1798	.0403	1828	.0391
1739	.0398	1769	.0316	1799	.0403	1829	.0392
1740	.0398	1770	.0316	1800	.0403	1830	.0385
1741	.0398	1771	.0315	1801	.0403	1831	.0392
1742	.0398	1772	.0316	1802	.0426[5]	1832	.0385
1743	.0398	1773	.0336	1803	.0408	1833	.0387[8]
1744	.0398	1774	.0331	1804	.0397	1834	.0390
1745	.0398	1775	.0326	1805	.0388	1835	.0388
1746	.0326[5]	1776	.0326	1806	.0407	1836	.0388
1747	.0317	1777	.0320	1807	.0415	1837	.0388
1748	.0325	1778	.0334	1808	.0423	1838	.0388
1749	.0320	1779	.0342	1809	.0396[3]	1839	.0392
1750	.0317	1780	.0337	1810	.0396	1840	.0391
1751	.0322	1781	.0324	1811	.0396	1841	.0390[9]
1752	.0317	1782	.0319	1812	.0396	1842	.0388
1753	.0311	1783	.0319	1813	.0396	1843	.0387
1754	.0318	1784	.0336	1814	.0396	1844	.0388
1755	.0323	1785	.0350	1815	.0396	1845	.0386
1756	.0329	1786	.0344	1816	.0395[6]	1846	.0386
1757	.0330	1787	.0344	1817	.0404	1847	.0388
1758	.0320	1788	.0381	1818	.0413	1848	.0385
1759	.0326	1789	.0359	1819	.0426	1849	.0395[1]
1760	.0326	1790	.0382	1820	.0384[7]	1850	.0394

Sources:
1. N. W. Posthumus, *Inquiry into the History of Prices in Holland,* 2 vols. (Leiden, 1946-64), 1:490 ff.
2. Interpolation.
3. Par, or the mean equivalent of silver content during the year.
4. Par, as of 1 January.
5. *Parliamentary Papers,* 1810-11, x (43), pp. 197-228.
6. *PP,* 1819, iii (282), pp. 285-316.
7. *PP,* 1831-32, vi (722), pp. 588-97.
8. *PP,* 1840, iv (602), pp. 408-9.
9. *PP,* 1847-48, vii (395) (584), pp. 209-10.

10 | A NOTE ON WEIGHTS AND MEASURES

Since a number of systematic treatments of European historical weights and measures are available, as are others dealing specifically with West Africa, this note is confined to Senegambian variations on general systems.[1]

The fundamental unit of capacity throughout Senegambia and the western Sudan was the *mud* or *muul*, ultimately derived from the Arabic unit. In theory it was based on a fixed number of handfuls of grain (often 36, 40, or 48, depending on the region and the grain). Forty mud often made a larger unit called a *matar*, or 4 mud came to 1 *sawal*. The mud, however, was highly variable from region to region, though standardization began to come in the nineteenth century. The Senegalese government established the metric system for the colony in 1826, with official equivalents to the earlier system which standardized the matar at 70 liters and the mud (spelled *moule* in Senegalese French) at 1.75 liters. Later, Shaykh Umar took the standard of Nioro (48 handfuls or 4 liters) as the standard for the whole of the Umarian empire. Thus, the two moves toward standardization led to quite different sizes. See table A10.1.

The Senegalese standardization of 1826 also established the standard *barrique* or barrel at 280 liters. This measure was actually somewhat larger than the standard Bordeaux wine barrel at 226.6 liters, perhaps the most common measure in eighteenth-century France as well as England. The Senegalese barrique was also larger than the English hogshead of 238.5 liters, and it corresponded most closely to the *bourdeaux*, which the Gambian government standardized in the early nineteenth century at 8 English bushels or 290.8 liters.[2]

Conversions from measures of capacity to measures of weight are always troublesome, since no equivalent will be absolutely accurate under all circumstances of temperature and humidity. This becomes a problem in the gum trade, where Europeans dealt among themselves by weight but dealt with the Moors by capacity. The

Table A10.1. Sizes and Weights of the Senegambian *Mud* or *Moule*

Date	Place	Capacity	Weight
1685	Lake Rkiz, Mauritania	1.95 liters	
1819	Bundu	2 quarts (1.89 liters)	
1826	Senegal official capacity	1.75 liters	
1879	Fuuta Tooro	3 liters	
1847	Kaarta	1.5 liters	
1950's	Jawara (Mali) (36 handfuls of millet)	3 liters	2.5 kgs of millet
1892	Badon, eastern Senegal		1 kg of millet
1920's	Gidimaxa	4 liters	
1953	Bundu		3 kgs of millet
1950's	Not specified (Labouret)		2.25 kgs of millet
1890's	Soudan (present-day Mali) generally	2.5 liters	
c. 1910	Nioro (48 handfuls)	4 liters	

Sources: La Courbe, *Premier voyage*, p. 98; Gray, *Western Africa*, p. 196; Règlement de 19 juin 1826, *Bulletin administratif du Sénégal*, 1:133; P. Solliet, Report of 10 April 1879, ANS, 1 G 46; Raffenel, *Nouveau voyage*, 1:233; G. Boyer, "Un peuple de l'ouest soudanais: Les Diawara," *Mémoires de l'Institut français d'Afrique noire*, no. 29 (Dakar, 1953), pp. 111-12; A. Rançon, *Dans la haute Gambie: Voyage d'exploration scientifique 1891-92* (Paris, 1894), p. 409; J. H. Saint-Père, *Les Sarakollé du Guidimakha* (Paris, 1925), pp. 52-53; A. M. M'Bow, "Enquête préliminaire sur le village de Sénoudébou . . .," mimeographed (Dakar, 1954), p. 32; H. Labouret and others, *Le commerce extra-européen jusqu'aux temps modernes* (Paris, 1953), p. 109; C. Monteil, *Contes soudanais* (Paris, 1905), p. 21; Meniaud, *Haut-Sénégal-Niger*, 2:259-60.

Table A10.2. Changing Size of the Kantar in the Gum Trade

Date	Wt. of gum (kgms)	Authority
At first	108	Durand, *Sénégal*, 2:115
c. 1700	171 at escale du Désert 196 at Terrier Rouge	Labat, *Nouvelle relation*, p. 152
1718	220	"Mémoire général sur le commerce," ANF, C6 15
1719	234	Delcourt, *La France au Sénégal*, p. 387
1724	269	J. Demoin, "Extrait de la traite de gomme . . .," 10 August 1724, ANF, C6 8. (Also printed in Delcourt, pp. 382-87.)
1734	490	Règlements du Sénégal, 8 October 1734, ANF, C6 11
c. 1740	416	Price list of the Compagnie des Indes, ANF, C6 23
c. 1780	979	Golberry, *Travels*, 1:174
1783	1,077	Labarthe, *Voyage en Sénégal*, pp. 31, 188
1785-86	1,175	Durand, *Sénégal*, 2:115

usual measure was called the *kantar (quantar, quintal Maure),*
which had the disadvantage of being highly variable through time
as well as through space.[3] (See table A10.2.) Its tendency was
all in one direction, however, as it grew steadily from the seventeenth century to the nineteenth, when it was finally replaced by
weight. The new standard of the gum trade then came to be the
metricized livre of 0.5 kgs.

Gold was sold by weight throughout the period, the standard
being the ancient Islamic *mithqal,* which belongs to the ancient
family of weights in which 72 grains equal a mithqal (or *gros* in
French), 8 mithqal equal an ounce, 8 ounces equal a *marc* (in
French), and 2 marcs make a pound. The English system of Troy
weights belongs to that family, and three-twentieths of the Troy
ounce, or 72 Troy grains, is still exactly the weight of the
mithqal in many present-day Islamic systems.

The base of many of these systems was a specific number of actual seeds of a particular plant. Both the English Troy system
and many Islamic systems are based on barley grains weighing about
0.06479 grams each, while the grain at the base on the old French
weighed 0.05311 grams, and that at the base of the English avoirdupois system weighed 0.05906.

The mithqal of Senegambia and its hinterland eastward to Bambuhu
and the Bure gold fields (and still used in Western Mauritania)
was somewhat smaller than the usual Islamic mithqal, since it fell
within the range of 3.7 to 4.0 grams. It was based on a seed
(probably that of the *acacia albida*) which is larger than the
seeds used in the Mediterranean basin. Only 6 seeds made the
weight of the mithqal of 3.7 to 4 grams. By coincidence, however, the 72 seeds of the French system yielded a gros of 3.825
grams, a weight so close to the Senegambian mithqal that the two
merged in Senegambian usage.

Meanwhile, the more common mithqal based on 72 seeds or English
troy grains yielded a mithqal of 4.665 grams, and weights in this order
of magnitude and slightly more were common in the Niger bend and
eastward toward Lake Chad. In the greater Manding culture area
the ordinary mithqal tended to be about 4.5 grams, with an approximate line of division that would put Bure and Bambuhu in the Senegambian mithqal area, while the area of the Manding mithqal extended westward along the *sahal* to take in Gajaaga and Gidimaxa.[4]

While the Senegambian mithqal merged neatly with French weights,
and the Manding mithqal would have merged reasonably well with
English Troy weights, the English traders on the Gambia found
that their avoirdupois system fitted better to the Senegambian
standard. One dram avoirdupois was 1.772 grams, so that two drams
came to 3.543 grams—only about 7 per cent less than the Senegambian
mithqal. It seems likely that the Royal African Company, which
kept its records in drams, actually bought its gold using the
mithqal of the country and accepted this degree of error.

Heavier products were commonly treated in units that were nearly
equal between French and English systems. Ivory, wax, and the
like were dealt with as though the French *quintal* of 100 livres
(48.95 kgs) were equal to an English hundredweight of 112 pounds
(50.8 kgs). In the same way, brandy or rum were bought from the
Europeans without troubling whether the unit was the *pinte de*

Paris at 0.931 liters or the English quart at 0.946 liters.

Measures of length were also easily coordinated between the English, French, and Senegambian systems, since all three were based on the same measures of the human body as the inch, foot, span, fathom, and so on. The most common Senegambian measure of length, for example, was the distance from the elbow to the fingertips, which was easily assimilated to a half-yard or to 0.5 meters.

NOTES

1. For European weights and measures see H. Doursther, *Dictionnaire universel des poids et mesures anciens et modernes* (1840; reprinted, Amsterdam, 1965), and R. D. Zupko, *A Dictionary of English Weights and Measures from Anglo-Saxon Times to the Nineteenth Century* (Madison, 1968). For the western Sudan generally see M. Johnson, "The Nineteenth-Century Gold 'Mithqal' in West and North Africa," *JAH*, 9:547-69 (1968); R. Mauny, *Tableau géographique de l'ouest africain au moyen age* (Dakar, 1961), pp. 410-26; J. Meniaud, *Haut-Sénégal-Niger: Géographie économique*, 2 vols. (Paris, 1912), 2:257-64. In so far as possible, Doursther has been taken as the preferred authority for conversions to metric weights and measures in the foregoing chapters.

2. Brooks, *Yankee Traders*, p. 184.

3. Most European sources treat the quintal maure and the qantar as identical, though one (P. Labarthe, *Voyage en Sénégal pendant les années 1784 et 1785, d'après les mémoires de Lajaille* (Paris, 1802), pp. 30-31) distinguished, probably mistakenly, between a Moorish quintal weighing about 900 French livres in gum as of 1783, and the qantar, weighing about 2,200 livres.

11 | PRINCIPAL OVERSEAS EXPORTS

A critique of the various quantity estimates for the slave trade from Senegambia is found in chapter 4, but data claimed to be an actual count of the number exported are available for the English trade to the Gambia in only one year (1766-67). French-carried exports are recorded for only fifteen years of the whole period 1680-1830, and these reports, given in table A11.1,

Table A11.1. French Slave Exports from Senegambia Recorded Annually

Year or period	No. exported	Annual rate	No. landed in America	No. of ships	Slaves per ship
15 Aug 1715 to					
13 February 1716[1]	1,190	(2,380)	---	5	238
31 July 1726 to[2]					
31 March 1732		(858)	4,854	---	---
1732[3]	1,039	1,039		4	260
1733	1,124	1,124		3	375
1734	833	833		2	417
1735	684	684		2	342
1736	670	670		2	335
1737	1,207	1,207		3	402
1738	869	869		2	435
1739	1,195	1,195		3	398
1740	1,152	1,152		2	576
1732-1740	8,773	1,097	8,160	23	381
1784[4]		1,071			
1786		1,683			
1787		1,722			
1788		1,988			

Sources:
1. Brüe to CI, 13 February 1716, ANF, C6 5.
2. "Etat" dated 28 July 1732, ANF, C6 10. Number is total number shipped by the Compagnie des Indes.
3. "Sénégal de 1731 à 1740," ANF C6 12. Number is the trade of the Compagnie des Indes.
4. Statistical reports for these years in ANF, C6 19. Numbers are of slaves purchased and shipped from Saint Louis and Gorée, which would include Gambia slaves using Gorée as an entrepôt, but not direct shipments from the Gambia.

are at least a point of departure for other estimates. Other exports were often recorded in some detail, though in widely scattered sources. Some of these data have been discussed in the text, but often in aggregates larger than the annual export record or estimate. They are therefore assembled here on an annual basis. Quantities are translated from earlier measures into metric units. The data claim to be actual measures of exports unless they are marked *c*, meaning a capacity measure or estimate of the expected or usual performance. A single set of source notes at the end of this appendix refers to all commodities, but lettered notes will appear after each section in turn. Reference to the year indicates all data for that year which are not otherwise annotated.

GOLD (KGMS)[a]

Year	Shipped from					Total
	St. Louis	Gajaaga	Gorée	Gambia by French	by English	
1687[1]	c 1.7[b]	2.9[2]	---		c 6.7	c 8.4
1693[3]	c 9.1		c 1.2		c 24.5	c 34.8
1698[4]	---	c 6.9	---		---	
1718[5]	---	c 12.3	---		---	
1723[6]		c 12.3				
1730[7]		15.4				
1733[8]		c 24.5				
1737[9]	---	20.1				
1740[10]		25.8				
1751[11]		24.5				
1757[12]		c 55.1				
1786[13,14]	---	2.6	---			
1788	---	3.3[15]	---		---	
1820	---	0.3[16]	---		---	
1822	---	1.0[17]	---		---	
1823	---	---	---		70.3[18]	
1826	---	3.94[19]	---		---	

Gold (continued)

Year	Shipped from					Total
	St. Louis	Gajaaga	Gorée	Gambia		
				by French	by English	
1828	---	1.0[17]	---	---	20.7[20]	
1829	---	5.1[21]	---	---	18.9[20]	
1830	---	5.0[21]	---	---	c 14.2[22]	
1832	---	40.3[23]	---	---	22.7[20]	
1833	---	---	---	---	32.3[20]	
1834	---	2.3[17]	---	---	1.2[20]	
1835	---	---	---	---	8.1[20]	
1836[24]	---	50.2	---	---	35.5	85.7
1837[24]	91.4	0.6[17]	---	---	---	
1838	---	0.8[17]	---	---	8.6[20]	
1839	---	0.9[17]	---	---	9.5[20]	
1840	---	0.4[17]	---	---	9.1[20]	
1841	---	---	---	---	32.1[20]	
1842	---	1.4[17]	---	---	1.7[20]	
1843	---	2.3[17]	---	---	2.2[20]	
1844	---	66.0[24]	---	---	9.7[20]	91.7
1845	86.0[25]	2.3[17]	---	---	5.7[20]	
1846	84.9[25]	2.9[17]	---	---	---	
1850	---	---	---	---	0.8[20]	

a. It should be remembered that gold statistics are markedly less accurate than others for this period, partly because gold was easy to hide from customs inspection and partly because it was not always counted as a commodity.

b. *Sic*. Gajaaga gold was normally shipped through Saint Louis, which suggests that the Saint Louis estimate is simply wrong for this year. It may be so, but it could also be taken as a representative figure for any year about this time.

GUM (METRIC TONS)

The gum export totals listed here cannot be taken as the total export of the Mauritanian-Senegalese gum-producing region because of the unlisted imports that might also flow in any year through the ports on the Mauritanian coast. English and French both traded there when they did not hold Saint Louis, and the Dutch were occasionally in that trade as well. At times, however, the Mauritania gum exports will appear as part of the exports (actually re-exports) of Gorée or Bathurst. This was especially true of the early nineteenth century, when many of the most active merchants in the Atlantic coastal gum trade were Afro-Europeans from Bathurst.

Gum indicated as exported from Saint Louis could also have been purchased at the lower-Senegal *escales* or in Gajaaga; the upriver centers of gum purchase were sometimes indicated and sometimes not. When upriver sources are not indicated, the Saint Louis figure can usually be taken to be the total gum export for the whole river valley.

Year	Saint Louis	Escales	Gajaaga	Gambia	Total
1687[1]	49	---	---	--	49
1688[26]	773				773
1693[3]	c. 196				1,175[a]
1718[5]	59	49	---	---	108
1723[6]	c. 392	---	---	---	392
1733[8]	490	---	---	---	490
1740[10]	387	---	---	---	387
1743[27]	1,439	---	---	---	1,439
1745	c. 538	---	---	---	c. 538
1746[28]	1,322	---	---	---	1,322
1754[29]	261	---	---	---	261
1756[28b]	175	---	---	---	175[b]
1757[29]	500	---	---	---	500
1773[30]	305[c]	---	---	---	305[c]
1777[31]	c. 695[d]	---	---	---	c. 695[d]
1781[32]	c. 196	---	---	---	196
1784[33]	---	---	339	---	---
1786[13]	95[e]	---	---	---	---
1787[34]	447	---	---	---	447
1788[48]	300	---	---	---	300
1789[33]	527	---	---	---	527
1790[33]	523	---	---	---	523
1791[31]	518	---	---	---	518
1794[35]	84[f]	---	---	---	84[f]
1795[35]	348[f]	---	---	---	348[f]
1796[35]	336[f]	---	---	---	336[f]
1797[35]	273[f]	---	---	---	273[f]
1798[35]	420[f]	---	---	---	420[f]
1799[35]	543[f]	---	---	---	543[f]
1802[35]	952[f]	---	---	---	952[f]
1810[36]	1,016	---	---	---	---
1817[37]	536	---	---	---	536
1818	688	---	---	---	688
1820[17]	---	---	20	---	---
1821[17]	---	---	257	---	---
1822[38]	---	754	125	---	879
1823[39]	150	761	c. 150	5[18]	1,066
1824[40]	---	1,164	103	---	1,267
1825[41]	614	---	---	---	614

(continued)

Year	Saint Louis	Escales	Gajaaga	Gambia	Total
1826[41]	---	1,104[g]	156	---	1,260
1827[42]	1,098	---	---	---	1,098
1828[42]	---	1,565[g]	218	110[20]	2,001
1829[42]	---	1,186[g]	202	89[20]	1,477
1830[42]	---	1,313[g]	399	3[20]	1,715
1831[42]	---	1,582[g]	394[17]	18[20]	1,994
1832[42]	1,793	---	---	---	---
1833[24]	1,202	---	---	279[20]	1,481
1834[24]	---	871[g]	221[17]	266[20]	1,162
1835[24]	1,413	---	---	138[20]	1,551
1836[24]	1,791	---	---	218[20]	2,009
1837[24]	---	2,464[g]	412[17]	---	2,876
1838[24]	---	3,912[g]	303[17]	366[20]	4,581
1839[24]	---	3,747[g]	117[17]	379[20]	4,243
1840[24]	---	2,816[g]	157[17]	24[20]	2,997
1841[24]	2,231	---	---	6[20]	2,237
1842[24]	---	802	401[17]	3[20]	1,206
1843[24]	430[h]	511[43]	167[17]	92[20]	1,200
1844[24]	---	1,028[43]	317[i]	55[20]	1,400
1845[43]	---	2,957	792	96[20]	3,845
1846[43]	---	2,218	531	217[20]	2,966
1847[43]	---	1,621	644	8[20]	2,273
1848[43]	---	798	856	---[j]	---[j]
1849[43]	---	1,175	996	32[25]	2,203
1850[24]	---	579[43]	683[i]	---	1,262

a. Includes 979 tons loaded at Portendick.
b. Figure reported is the annual average for the period 1752-62.
c. Exports from the whole Province of Senegambia, which included the Gambia as well as Fort Lewis at the mouth of the Senegal.
d. Estimate for the period of English occupation of Saint Louis generally, that is approximate annual average for 1759-78.
e. This is the official export figure, supposedly measured. It conflicts with estimates of 739 tons by authority referred to in note 13 below, and 176 tons by authority in note 79.
f. Not the present calendar year but the years of the French revolutionary calendar, An II listed as 1794 to An VII listed as 1799. Data listed under 1802 is actually that for the last six months of An X and the first six months of An XI.
g. Since little or no gum was traded in Saint Louis itself, the difference between the recorded Gajaaga exports and the total should equal the exports by way of the *escales*.
h. If the data reported for the *escales* and for Gajaaga are accurate, this much had to come from Saint Louis, if the total is also accurate, but it could also result from an error in any of the three recorded figures.
i. When the total and the exports from the *escales* were recorded, the difference should represent the exports from Gajaaga.
j. No Gambia data for this year, therefore the assumption of no trade by way of the Gambia cannot be made.

HIDES (HUNDREDS)

The one statistical problem proper to the hide trade is the fact that the English measured hides by the unit, as did the French until 1833, when they switched to metric tons. No single number of units per ton can be accurate in all cases, but a comparison of prices in the Gambian and Senegalese customs-house usage after 1833 suggests that hides at that time came to about 195 per ton. This conversion factor is used for the conversion of the Senegalese data for 1817-18 and 1833-50 from metric tons to hundreds of hides.

Year	By French, all regions	By English, from Gambia	Total
c. 1594[44]	60-70	---	---
1590[44]	---	140[a]	---
1606[44]	---	---	300-350[b]
1616[44]	---	---	500[c]
1647[44]	---	---	700[d]
c. 1660[44]	350-400	500	1,500[e]
1676[44]	---	---	800[f]
1677[45]	---	c. 100	---
1679-80[46]	---	260	---
1683[47]	---	151	---
1684[47]	---	78	---
1685[47]	---	103	---
1686[47]	---	102	---
1687[47]	---	90	c. 275[1]
1688[47]	c. 100[26]	82	c. 182
1693[3]	c. 135	300	c. 435
1718[5]	c. 48	---	---
1723[6]	c. 100	---	---
1740[10]	6	---	---
1786[34]	1	---	---
1787[34]	6	---	---
1788[48]	8	---	---
1794[35]	4	---	---
1795[35]	4	---	---
1796[35]	3	---	---
1799[35]	9		
1802[49]	16		
1811[36]	250		
1817[50]	8		
1818[50]	20		
1822[38]	168		
1823		837[18]	
1824[40]	482		
1825[41]	389		
1826[41]	260	659[20]	919
1829		604[20]	
1830[20]		765	
1831[20]		660	

Year	Saint Louis	Gajaaga	Gorée	Gambia	Total
1832	2,690[24]	---[g]	---[g]	715[h]	3,405
1833	1,135[24]	---[g]	---[g]	769[20]	1,904
1834	891[24]	20[17]	---[g]	1,023[20]	1,934
1835	626[24]	---[g]	---[g]	950[h]	1,576
1836	452[24]	---[g]	---[g]	877[20]	1,329
1837	305[24]	5[17]	---[g]	905[20]	1,215
1838	470[24]	4[17]	---[g]	722[20]	1,196
1839	571[24]	4[17]	---[g]	895[20]	1,470
1840	638[24]	11[17]	---[g]	1,036[20]	1,685
1841	634[24]	---[g]	---[g]	738[20]	1,372
1842	739[24]	6[17]	---[g]	1,077[20]	1,822
1843	402[24]	21[17]	604[24]	987[20]	2,014
1844	339[24]	---[g]	456[24]	974[20]	1,769
1845	471[24]	20[17]	345[24]	977[20]	1,813
1846	253[24]	25[17]	450[24]	722[20]	1,350
1847	411[24]	---[g]	480[24]	834[20]	1,725
1848	135[24]	---[g]	196[24]	689[h]	1,020
1849	168[24]	---[g]	261[24]	543[20]	972
1850	216[24]	---[g]	318[24]	865[20]	1,399

a. Shipped by a single English ship.
b. Another estimate originating in the Cape Verde Islands was for 40,000 sides for this year.

    c. From the *petite côte* only, by all shippers.
    d. For Senegambia and the southern rivers combined, but supposed to be mainly Senegambia.
    e. Total included 60,000 annually shipped from the *petite côte* by the Dutch.
    f. *Petite côte* only, all shippers, including English trade with entrepôt at the Gambia.
    g. Included under Saint Louis.
    h. Interpolation.

IVORY (METRIC TONS)

Ivory was not a homogeneous product with a value proportionate to its weight. In the 1680's and again in the 1730's (and probably in the years between), the large tusks in the vicinity of 25 to 35 kgs each brought a little more than twice the price of small tusks around 5 kgs or less each. After about 1741, however, the Senegambian literature has little to say about differential prices, and the customs records of the nineteenth century treat ivory by weight and at an undifferentiated price.

Year	Shipped from					Total
	St. Louis	Gajaaga	Gorée	Gambia by French	by English	
1677[45]					c. 14.2	
1679-80[46]					12.0	
1683			c. 7.3		31.0[47]	41.8
1684					11.0[47]	
1685					23.0[47]	
1686					19.0[47]	
1687	c. 9.8	---	c. 4.9	c. 27.2[a]	20.0[47]	c. 63.7
1688					24.0[47]	
1693[3]	c. 13.2	---	c. 7.3	c. 14.7[b]		c. 35.2
1707					76.1	
1718[5]	---	c. 1.0	c. 0.5	c. 9.8		
1723[6]	c. 19.6[c]					
1733[8]	c. 4.8[d]					
1740[10]	0.3[c]					
1741[37]					c. 25.4	
1757[12]	c. 14.0[c] [e]					
1773[30]					c. 4.1[f]	
1786[13]	10.1[51]	2.0[51]	---[g]	c. 0.5	c. 24.6	c. 37.0
1787[34]	5.4[c]					
1788	1.1[48]	3.2[15]	---[g]		c. 9.1	c. 12.5
1794[35]	0.9[c]					
1795[35]	5.6[c]					
1796[35]	2.9[c]					
1797[35]	0.2[c]					
1798[35]	0.7[c]					
1799[35]	12.5[c]					
1802[49]	1.3[c]					
1817[37]	1.5[c]					
1820[16]		1.1				
1821[17]		1.1				
1822[38]	0.3	1.9[17]	---[g]			

(continued)

Ivory (continued)

Year	Shipped from					Total
	St. Louis	Gajaaga	Gorée	Gambia		
				by French	by English	
1823	3.9[h]				8.8[18]	12.7
1824[40]	5.6				8.3	13.9
1825[41]	6.4	---[g]				
1826[41]	8.2	3.5[17]				
1828		3.3[17]				
1829		4.9[17]			5.8[21]	
1830		3.0[17]			6.6[22]	
1831					10.7[20]	
1832	13.4[24]				12.3[20]	25.7
1833	13.3[h]				13.3[20]	26.6
1834	13.2[24]	2.3[17]	---[g]		13.3[20]	28.8
1835[24]	12.3[c]				15.6[h]	27.9
1836	12.2[24] c				17.8[20]	30.0
1837	27.3[24]	0.7[17]	---[g]		13.9[20]	41.9
1838	13.2[24] c				9.3[20]	22.5
1839	8.1[24]	0.9[17]	---[g]		12.2[20]	21.2
1840	6.8[24]	0.2[17]	---[g]		10.6[20]	17.6
1841	6.0[24] c				12.7[20]	18.7
1842	4.5[24]	0.5[17]	---[g]		6.0[20]	11.0
1843[24]	1.5	0.9[17]	3.1		5.8[20]	11.3
1844[24]	1.7	---[g]	4.0		7.2[20]	12.9
1845[24]	2.4	1.6[17]	4.3		10.7[20]	19.0
1846[24]	1.6	1.9[17]	3.8		5.3[20]	12.6
1847[24]	2.9	---[g]	2.0		4.3[20]	9.2
1848[24]	2.4	---[g]	4.8		3.5[h]	10.7
1849[24]	2.2	---[g]	---		2.7[20]	4.9
1850[24]	2.4	---[g]	0.7		2.1[20]	5.2

a. The estimated French export from Gambia derived from the estimated value of all Gambia exports less the actual measure of English exports.
b. All Gambian exports regardless of carrier.
c. All exports carried by French, regardless of the point of shipment.
d. Two and sixty-nine hundredths in large tusks plus 2.08 in small tusks.
e. Estimate for an ordinary year before the French loss of Saint Louis to the English.
f. Annual average for 1769-1778.
g. Included with figures for Saint Louis.
h. Interpolation.

BEESWAX (METRIC TONS)

Year	Shipped from					Total
	St. Louis	Gajaaga[a]	Gorée	Gambia		
				by French	by English	
1677[45]					c. 14	
1679-80[46]					8	
1683[47]					23	
1684[47]					10	
1685[47]					11	
1686[47]					13	
1687[1]			c. 5	c. 16[b]	11[47]	c. 34

(continued)

Beeswax (continued)

Year	St. Louis	Gajaaga[a]	Gorée	Gambia by French	by English	Total
1688[47]						5
1693[3]			c. 7	c. 7[c]		c. 14
1707[52]					76	
1718[5]				c. 10		
1723[6]			c. 49[d]			
1733[8]			c. 10[d]			
1741[43]					114	
1757[15] e			4[e d]			
1773[30]			22[d f]			
1788[14]					30	
				Gambia		
1810[36]			61			
1817[37]			4[d]			
1822[38]	8					
1823				188[18]		
1824[40]			8[d]			
1825[40]	18					
1826[41]	43					
1827[50]				227[20]		
1828		1[17]		180[20]		
1829		2[17]		220[20]		
1830		2[17]		248[20]		
1831				6[20]		
1832				165[20]		
1833[24]			78[d]	178[20]		256
1834[24]			84[d]	193[20]		277
1835[24]			44[d]	254[20]		298
1836[24]			45[d]	255[20]		300
1837[24]			24	210[20]		234
1838[24]			51[d]	237[20]		288
1839[24]			81[d]	248[20]		329
1840[24]			47[d]	290[20]		337
1841[24]			124[d]	204[20]		328
1842[24]			102[d]	298[20]		400
1843[24]	22	1[17]	133	260[20]		416
1844[24]	23	---	118	214[20]		355
1845[24]	16	---	82	209[20]		306
1846[24]	13	---	76	274[20]		363
1847[24]	21	---	206	306[20]		533
1848[24]	24	---	146	---		367[g]
1849[24]	15	---	52	134[20]		201
1850[24]	5	---	60	279[20]		344

a. Gajaaga shipped small quantities less than .5 tons in several years. See appendix 12 below.

b. Estimate for all Gambia, less British exports.

c. All Gambia, regardless of the nationality of carrier.

d. All French, regardless of the shipping point

e. Estimate for an ordinary year before the British capture of Saint Louis.

f. Annual average for 1769-78.

g. Interpolation.

PEANUTS (METRIC TONS)

Both prices and quantities of peanuts exported are uncertain for the early years, because of possible confusion between decorticated and undecorticated. Senegalese data before 1850 never specify; Gambian data specify only for some years. The undecorticated portion

of the Gambian exports was always 80 per cent or more of the total value during these years, which gives some idea of the possible range of error. In the table below, unspecified exports are
treated as undecorticated.

Year		Shipped from				Total
	St. Louis[24]	Gajaaga[17]	Gorée[17]	Gambia[20]		
				decorticated	undecorticated	
1831					3	3
1834					2	2
1835					49	49
1836					132	132
1837					682	682
1838					679	679
1839				72	824	896
1840	1[a]			85	1,146	1,232
1841	259[a]			31	2,341	2,631
1842	1,012[a]			187	2,184	3,383
1843	193	4	796[b]	93	2,630	3,716
1844	113	---[c]	861	441	3,040	4,455
1845	186	---[c]	411	450	3,591	4,638
1846	204	1	797	341	5,752	7,095
1847	1,135	---[c]	563	139	8,230	10,067
1848	1,993	---[c]	1,181	76[d]	6,313[d]	9,563
1849	3,175	---[c]	431	13	4,396	8,015
1850	2,600	---[c]	45	---	6,105	8,750

a. Total French exports regardless of shipping point.
b. Source gives 4,063 tons, but this is so far from probability in comparison
with other data that it is set aside in favor of an interpolation.
c. Included under Saint Louis.
d. Interpolation

APPENDIX SOURCES

1. Ducasse, "Mémoire ou relation du S. du Casse sur son voyage
de Guinée," (Mss., AN-OM, DFC Senegal 1, no. 4).
2. Poncet de la Rivière to MC, 25 May 1764, ANF, C6 15.
3. LaCourbe, "Mémoire sur le commerce de Guinée," ANF, C6 2.
4. Bruë to Collé, 9 Dec. 1716, ANF, C6 5.
5. Unsigned, undated, "Mémoire général sur le commerce du
Sénégal," ANF, C6 14. Data reprinted, identified as 1718 in
Postlethwayt, *Universal Dictionary* (1751), 1:845.
6. Unsigned, "Mémoire sur le commerce du Sénégal," 11 October
1723, ANF, C6 7.
7. Statement of Account, dated 1 August 1731, ANF, F2 A 13.
8. Levens, Memorandum of 16 August 1733, ANF, C6 10.
9. Conseil du Sénégal to CI, 28 January 1738, C6 11.
10. "Etat de la dépense général de la concession du 1ère juin
1738 au 31e mai 1740," ANF, C6 12, an annual average for two years
of actual performance.
11. "Notes prises avec M. de la Bruë," 18 July 1751, ANF,
C6 12.

12. M. Adanson, "Pièces instructives concernant l'isle de Gorée," ANF, C6 15.

13. Memorandum on Exports, ANF, C6 19.

14. Evidence of Captain Heatley, *Board of Trade Report*, part 1.

15. "Voyage de Galam, 1788," ANF, C6 19.

16. Saulnier, *Compagnie de Galam*, p. 48.

17. Saulnier, appendix 1. All of these are fiscal years bridging two calendar years. Totals are listed under the second of the two years.

18. J. Rowan, Report of 9 June 1827, CO 267/93, p. 9.

19. Enclosure in despatch of Governor of Senegal to MC, 16 December 1826, ANF-OM, Sénégal XIII 7. Figures are for the year 1 Nov. 1825 to 31 October 1826.

20. Gambia Blue Books, annual series, CO 90.

21. Bruë to Saint-Germain, Saint Louis, 31 March 1831, ANS, 13 G 22.

22. Belcher, "Extracts," *JRGS*, 2:296-97.

23. Saulnier, p. 61.

24. France, Ministère des colonies, *Statistiques coloniales . . .* (Paris, 1832-96), annual series.

25. Exports from Saint Louis only (not including Gorée). ANF-OM, Sénégal XIII 72.

26. Chambonneau to Marquis de Signalay, June 1688, ANF, Col. C6 1.

27. Conseil du Sénégal to CI, 15 July 1743, ANF, C6 12.

28. Unsigned memorandum of 2 Nov. 1762, quoted by Machat, *Documents*, p. 82.

29. Le Bart to CI, 3 November 1757, ANF, C6 14.

30. William Rogers, Memorandum dated 29 August 1778, CO 267/17, giving the estimates by "competent judges" of the annual average purchases in the Province of Senegambia over the period approximately 1769-78.

31. Unsigned "Mémoire sur le commerce du Sénégal," February 1783, ANF, C6 18.

32. "Mémoire du roi . . . au Sieur Demontent," 1 April 1782, Shefer, *Instructions générals*, 1:88-90.

33. Labarthe, *Voyage en Sénégal*, pp. 179-180.

34. Exportation du Sénégal et Gorée, 1786-87," ANF, C6 19.

35. "Renseignements sur le Sénégal," ANF, C6 27, pp. 225-26.

36. Exports shipped from Gorée and Saint Louis under British occupation. Maxwell, Answers to Commissioners, 1 January 1811, CO 267/29.

37. "Mémoire concernant le commerce," enclosed with Commander, Gorée, to Director, Saint Louis, 4 June 1741, AN, C6 12.

38. "Situation de la Place de Saint-Louis, 30 December 1822," ANF-OM, Sénégal XIII 72.

39. "Situation de la Place à Saint-Louis, 3 August 1828," ANF-OM, Senegal XIII 72.

40. Statement dated 9 August 1825, ANF-OM, Sénégal XIII 72.

41. Statistical survey in ANS, 22 G 3.

42. Duchon-Dorix, *Toiles bleus*, p. 64. Since these figures are mainly derived from French records of imports from Senegal, they do not agree perfectly with the Senegalese records of

exports; but they are used for years when the Senegalese records are missing.

43. Documents no. 6 and 7, ANF-OM, Sénégal XIII 72. The Saint Louis figure is the total of the two indicating the point of trade, Gajaaga or *escales*.

44. Data assembled by Jean Boulègue, "Luso-Africains," pp. 41-43.

45. Thomas Thurloe to RAC, Gambia, 14 March 1677-78, in Donnan, *Documents*, 1:234.

46. Davies, *Royal African Company*, p. 219, 6-months totals doubled for annual rate.

47. Quantities exported from British Gambia calculated from Gambia accounts of the RAC in T 70/546. See appendix 15, pp. 86-87 for the method of calculation.

48. Statistical reports in ANF, C6 19.

49. Statement covering second half of the year X and the first half of the year XI (approximately March 5, 1802, to March 4, 1803), ANF, C6 20.

50. France, Direction générale des duanes, *Tableau décennal du commerce de la France*. *Volume I, 1827-46* (Paris, 1848). Figures are imports into France from Senegal, including reexports from France. Since all Senegalese exports were legally supposed to go to France, except for hides and dyewoods, these figures should be at least roughly the same as total Senegalese exports.

51. Memorandum dated 17 May 1787, ANF, C6 19, an actual record of purchases, not a capacity estimate.

52. Extract of despatch from Thomas Adcock to RAC, 28 June 1707, T 70/5.

12 | RETURN CARGOES, GAJAAGA TO SAINT LOUIS, ANNUAL HIGH-WATER EXPEDITIONS

Contrary to the usual situation, where the internal and overland movement of goods goes unrecorded, data on river traffic downstream between Gajaaga on the upper Senegal and St. Louis at the mouth of the river are remarkably complete for certain stretches of time and in regard to certain commodities. This is especially the case for the movement of slaves in the early eighteenth century and for the movement of gum and other "legitimate" products in the early nineteenth. In this case, however, as with other figures on exports by sea from Senegambia, those having to do with gold shipments are especially unreliable.

Year	Boats (no.)	Crew (no.)	Slaves (no.)	Wax (tons)	Gold (kgs)	Ivory (tons)	Cotton (tons)
1686	---	---	15				
1688?	---	---	50	---	2.9[1]		
1690	---	---	116				
1691-93[2]	---	---	---	---	---	---	---
1698[3]	---	---	248	---	18.0	some	
1699	---	---	---	---	---	---	---
1702	---	---	---				---
1703-6[4]	---	---	---	---	---	---	---
1707[5]	---	---	---	---	---	---	---
1708-9	---	---	---	---	---	---	
1710[6]	---	---	113	---	3.7		
1712?	---	---	---	---	---	---	---
1718[7]	---	---	---	---	12.2		
1720[8]	---	---	>300				
1722[9]	---	---	419				
1724	---	---	350[10]	---	0.3[11]		
1732[12]	---	---	300				
1733[13]	---	---	1,124				
1737[14]	---	---	>131	---	20.1		
1738[15]	---	---	200		19.6		
1741[16]	---	---	>900				
1742[17]	---	---	1,500				
1743[18]	---	---	1,100				
1744[19]	19						
1745	---	---	450				
1750[20]	---	---	475				
1751[21]	---	---	120				
1753[22]	---	---	448				
1754[23]	---	---	550				
1755[24]	---	---	350	---	---	---	---
1756[25]	---	---	200	---	---	---	---
1757	40	---	213	---	---	---	---
1762[26]	---	---	---	---	---	---	---
1763-64	---	---	---	---	---	---	---
1770-76[27]	---	---	---	---	---	---	---
1784[28]	---	---	---	---	3.1	2.1	---
1785	27	350					
1786[29]	22	---	766	---	2.6	2.0	
1787[30]	---	---	---	---	---	---	---
1788[31]	43	---	964	---	3.3	3.2	
1790[32]	---	---	---	---	---	---	---
1791[33]	---	---	450	---	---	---	---
1799[34]	---	---	---	---	---	---	---
1803-11	---	---	---	---	---	---	---
1812-16[35]	---	---	---	---	---	---	---
1812[36]	75	c 1,000	---	---	35.0	3.5	---
1817	---	---	---	---	---	---	---
1818	---	---	---	---	---	---	---
1819-20[37]	---	---	---	---	---	---	---
1820-21	---	---	---	---	0.3	1.1	0.5
1821-22	---	---	---	---	1.0	1.9	---
1823-24	---	---	---	---	---	---	---
1825-26	---	---	118	0.2	3.9[39]	3.5	---
1827-28	---	---	---	1.4	1.0	3.3	---

(continued)

Gum (tons)	Hides (tons)	Peanuts (tons)	Millet (tons)	Remarks

---	---	---	---	No voyage these years

---	---	---	---	Upriver post established
---	---	---	---	Post of Dramane evacuated
---	---	---	---	No voyage these years
---	---	---	---	Renewed voyage attempted, but failed to reach Gajaanga
---	---	---	---	No voyage these years

---	---	---	---	Post founded at Maxaana

---	---	---	---	Estimate for "before 1744"

---	---	---	---	Estimate for 1745-58

---	---	---	24.5	
---	---	---	200.0	
---	---	---	---	Beginning of evacuation of all-season posts in Gajaaga
---	---	---	---	Evacuation completed
---	---	---	---	Prosperous trade
---	---	---	---	Trade with Gajaaga very small

---	---	---	---	No fleet, as a result of high Futaanke demands for tolls
---	---	---	---	No voyage to Gajaaga that year
---	---	---	---	Voyage reached only as far as Salde in Fuuta
---	---	---	---	Voyage this year
---	---	---	---	No voyage
---	---	---	---	Regular voyages resumed during English occupation[35]
---	---	---	300.0	
---	---	---	---	Voyage failed to reach Gajaaga
---	---	---	---	Voyages resumed
10.0	---	---	---	Here and below, double years are a single fiscal year unless otherwise indicated
157.5				
125.0[38]				
102.5				
156.3				
218.4				

Return Cargoes (continued)

Year	Boats (no.)	Crew (no.)	Slaves (no.)	Wax (tons)	Gold (kgs)	Ivory (tons)	Cotton (tons)
1828-29	---	---	18[40]	1.8	5.1[41]	4.9	---
1829-30	---	---	---	1.5	5.0[41]	3.0	---
1830-31	---	---	220[42]	---	---	---	---
1832	---	---	---	---	40.3[43]	---	---
1833-34	88	1,200[44]	---	---	2.3	8.4	---
1836-37	---	---	---	---	0.6	2.7	---
1837-38	---	---	---	---	0.8	0.7	---
1838-39	---	---	---	---	0.9	0.9	---
1839-40	---	---	---	---	0.4	0.2	---
1841-42	---	---	---	---	1.4	0.5	---
1842-43	---	---	---	0.8	2.3	0.9	---
1844-45	---	---	---	0.2	2.4	1.6	---
1845-46	---	---	---	0.3	2.9	1.9	---
1848-49	30[28]	---	---	---	---	---	---
1850-51	---	---	---	---	---	---	---
1851-52	---	---	---	0.7	2.4	0.6	---
1852-53	---	---	---	0.1	0.3	0.4	---
1845-49[45]	---	---	---	17.5	86.9	3.0	---

Sources:

1. Chambonneau to Compagnie du Sénégal, quoted in Froidveaux, "Découverte du Félou," p. 310.

2. LaCourbe, "Mémoire sur le commerce," 26 March 1693, ANF, C6 3; also printed in *Premier voyage*, p. iii.

3. Labat, *Nouvelle relation*, 3:336, supposedly based on the journal of André de la Bruë, though De la Bruë himself remembered in 1716 that he had bought some 400 slaves, and at that time specified the amount of gold listed for 1698. (Bruë to Collé, BN, FF, NA, 9341, f. 42.)

4. Labat, *Nouvelle relation*, 4:22-31.

5. John Snow to RAC, 9 August 1707, T 70/5.

6. LaCourbe to CI, 30 January 1709, ANF, C6 3.

7. Unsigned "Mémoire sur le commerce du Sénégal," ANF, C6 14; same data published in M. Postlethwayt, *The Universal Dictionary of Trade and Commerce*, 2 vols. (London, 1751), 1:845.

8. Violaine to Director Saint Louis, 6 August 1720, ANF, C6 6.

9. Du Bellay to CI, 28 December 1722, ANF, C6 7.

10. Saint-Robert to CI, 18 July 1725, ANF, C6 9.

11. Charpentier to Director Saint Louis, 12 October 1772, ANF, C6 7.

12. Devaulx to CI, 28 May 1733, ANF, C6 10.

13. Boucard to Director Saint Louis, 1 April 1733, C6 10.

14. Conseil du Sénégal to CI, 14 August 1737 and 28 January 1738, ANF, C6 11.

15. Data are the numbers expected for current season, not performance. Conseil du Sénégal to CI, 30 June 1738, ANF, C6 11.

16. Conseil du Sénégal to CI, 14 January 1742, ANF, C6 12.

17. David to CI, 20 April 1743, ANF, C5 12.

18. "Mémoire sur le commerce du Sénégal," 2 November 1762, ANF, C6 14. Another document, undated but c. 1745, gives the slave-shipping capacity of Gajaaga as "up to 1,600" per year (ANF, C6 12).

19. Annotation of Labat text, ANF, C6 29.

20. "Extrait des lettres du Conseil du Sénégal," 8 January 1751, C6 13.

21. Conseil du Sénégal to CI, 30 July 1751, ANF, C6 13.

22. Conseil du Sénégal to CI, 12 February 1754, ANF, C6 14.

23. Conseil du Sénégal to CI, 31 July 1755, ANF, C6 14.

24. Conseil du Sénégal to CI, 15 March 1756, ANF, C6 14.

25. Conseil du Sénégal to CI, 2 March 1757, ANF, C6 14.

26. Aussenac to CI, 8 January 1759, ANF, C6 14; J. Tufton Mason despatch of 27 December 1758 and Richard Worge despatch of 19 October 1759, CO 267/12; J. Debat to R. Worge, James Fort, no date but c. late 1762, T 70/30.

27. J. P. Demairn to George Germaine, Fort Lewis, 4 July 1777, CO 267/16.

28. F. Deroure, "La vie quotidienne (1779-1809)," p. 404. L. P. Raybaud, "L'Administration du Sénégal de 1781 à 1784, *Annales africaines*, pp. 162, 171-72 (1968).

Gum (tons)	Hides (tons)	Peanuts (tons)	Millet (tons)	Remarks
202.1	---	---	---	Annual average these two years
398.7				
394.0				

221.0	10.3			
411.6	2.8	---	---	
303.2	---	---	---	
116.2	2.0	---	---	
146.8	5.6	---	---	
400.7	2.9	---	---	
167.1	10.7	4.3	---	
355.5	10.1	---	---	
358.9	12.7	0.6	---	
780.1	---	---	---	
929.9	---	---	---	
881.6	23.0	385.1	---	
1,172.9	63.2	1,007.6	---	
763.8	152.2	---	---	Annual average for these years

29. "Sénégal 1786: Voyage en Galam," ANF, C6 19.
30. Golberry, *Travels*, 1:184-86.
31. "Voyage de Galam 1788," ANF, col., C6 19.
32. Governor to MC, nos. 29 and 34, July 1790, ANF, C6 20.
33. Renseignements sur le Sénégal," ANF, C6 27, f. 180.
34. Blanchot to MC, 19 April 1800, ANF, C6 20.
35. J. P. Johnson, "The Almamate of Futa Toro, 1770-1836: A Political History" (Ph.D. diss., University of Wisconsin, 1974), chap. 6; Maxwell to Lord Liverpool, 9 March 1810, CO 267/33; Maxwell, Replies to H.M. Commissioners, 1 January 1811, CO 267/29.
36. A. A. Boahen, *Britain, the Sahara, and the Western Sudan 1788-1861* (Oxford, 1964), p. 36. Quantities are derived from calculating barrels of millet at approximately 200 kgs, and gold at the conventional price of £141 per kg.
37. Saulnier, *Compagnie de Galam*, appendix p. 187, is the authority for all data below this point, unless otherwise cited. Figure for this year is from Saulnier's text p. 48, which is preferred to a slightly different figure on his table p. 187.
38. Saulnier, *Compagnie de Galam*, p. 49. This is preferred to the figure in Roger to MC, 11 November 1833, ANF-OM, Sénégal, I.8.C, though the Roger figure is not significantly different. It is repeated with a copying error in Marty, *Etudes sénégalaises*, p. 189.
39. Memorandum enclosed with Governor to MC, 16 December 1826, ANF-OM, Sénégal XIII 7.
40. Financial accounts for the two calendar years 1828-29 shown here as an annual average. The slaves were bought for forcible enlistment in the French forces.
41. Bruë to Saint-Germain, Saint Louis, 31 March 1831, ANS, 13 G 22.
42. Rendale to Hay, Bathurst, no. 42, 3 August 1831, CO 87/5.
43. Of this total about 20 per cent was purchased by the Galam Company, the remainder by small traders. The figure is significant, since the reported data for gold were normally erroneous at this period and the figure here may well be closer to the actual amount bought each year. Saulnier, *Compagnie de Galam*, p. 61.
44. Governor to MC, 29 September 1834, ANS, 2 B 16.
45. Direction des colonies, "Commerce du Sénégal," 7 December 1850, ANF-OM, Sénégal XIII 2. These annual averages should be considered as more accurate than the spot figures located by Saulnier.

13 | "CUSTOMS" PAYMENTS IN SENEGAMBIA

Tolls collected from the individual merchant and payable according to the quantity of goods carried were quantitatively more significant than the formal gifts paid from government to government or by one of the European trading companies to African governments, though both were called customs. The amounts received by various Senegambian states are nevertheless some indication of interstate relations and their changes over time. The table that follows lists documented payments in particular years, and the sums paid can normally be taken to indicate the level of annual payment for an uncertain period before or after the date indicated. All payments are given as nearly as possible in the pound-sterling equivalent of the prime-cost value of the goods paid, rounded to the nearest pound. Payments by English authorities are italicized, the rest are French.

This table is very wide; columns left-to-right are: Date, French total, English total, Fuuta Tooro, Trarza, Waalo, Kajor, Bawol, Siin, Ñumi, Gajaaga, Xaaso, Bundu, Braknas, Idaw ʿAish.

Date	French total	English total	Fuuta Tooro	Trarza	Waalo	Kajor	Bawol	Siin	Ñumi	Gajaaga	Xaaso	Bundu	Braknas	Idaw ʿAish
1718	–	–	–	511	–	–	–	–	–	–	–	–	–	–
1722	257	–	170	–	–	–	–	–	–	42	–	–	–	81
1733	–	–	–	–	–	–	–	–	–	–	–	–	–	96
c. 1750's	–	–	–	–	–	70	–	–	–	–	–	–	–	–
1761	–	–	–	–	161	–	–	–	–	–	–	–	–	–
1764	–	–	159	200	161	–	–	–	–	–	–	–	–	–
1767	–	–	–	–	–	19	10	10	10	–	–	–	–	–
1768	–	–	–	–	–	19	51	25	38	–	–	69	–	–
1772	–	–	–	–	–	51	20	20	27	–	–	–	–	–
1773	–	–	–	–	–	20	–	48	61	–	–	–	–	–
1776	–	–	–	7	–	59	–	–	–	–	–	–	–	–
1777	–	–	–	–	–	46	–	33	72	49	14	–	–	–
1778	146	463	81	117	90	40	–	–	–	–	–	–	–	–
1779	–	–	172	–	–	41	41	32	27	–	34	–	–	–
1783	–	–	192	389	157	–	38[1]	32	26	–	27	–	–	–
1786	1,250[2]	–	211	–	–	113	–	–	–	123	–	211	–	–
1790	–	–	227	–	–	–	–	–	–	137	–	–	–	–
1791	–	–	–	–	–	–	–	–	–	151	–	–	–	–
1801	1,508	–	227	569	260	140	–	–	–	152	–	263	–	–
1809	–	1,430	–	–	–	–	–	–	–	–	–	–	–	–
1819	2,085	–	171	706	499	84	–	–	29	135	–	–	180	–
1828	1,688	–	157	512	418	137	–	–	–	166	–	–	137	–
1830	–	–	87	–	–	–	–	–	–	–	–	–	–	–
1834	–	396	–	–	–	–	–	–	–	–	–	–	–	–
1843	–	–	–	–	–	–	–	–	–	–	–	–	28	–
1849	–	–	–	–	–	–	–	–	–	–	–	–	–	316
1850	–	–	–	–	–	–	–	–	–	–	–	–	–	600
1853	–	–	–	–	–	–	–	–	–	–	–	–	–	980
1854	–	–	79	–	–	–	–	–	–	88	–	–	–	–

1. For both Kajor and Baol, not counting separate payment to Kajor from Saint Louis.
2. Including £85 paid from Gorée to unspecified authorities.

SOURCES

Levens, Mémoire of 16 August 1733, ANF, C6 10; C. Shefer, ed.,
*Instructions générales données de 1763 à 1870 aux gouverneurs et
ordonnateurs des établissements français en Afrique occidentale*,
2 vols. (Paris, 1921), 1:129; Annual returns 1773-79 in ANF,
C6 10; Mémoire du Roy au Sieur de Repentigny, 18 November 1783;
Shefer, *Instructions générales*, 1:123; J. B. L. Durand, *Sénégal*,
2:377-78; "Etat des dépenses au Sénégal, 1786, ANF, C6 19; "Etat
des presents et coutumes," 10 July 1801, ANF, C6 21; "Etat général
des coutumes, 1819, ANS, 13 G 16, and equivalent returns for 1829;
J. Huard to Bouët, 6 January 1844, ANF-OM, Sénégal III 6; J.
Barnes to Africa Committee, 17 February 1765, T 70/37; Julien de
Bellay to CI, 28 December 1722, ANF, C6 7; Brossard to Governor,
Médine, 29 October 1853, ANF-OM, Senegal IV 18; Rey to Governor,
Bakel, 10 April 1853 and 5 March 1851, ANS, 13 G 166; Cleziaud
to Grange et Cie., Bakel, 27 June 1853, ANS, 13 G 166.

14 | WAGES AND SALARIES IN THE TRADE ENCLAVES

Pay scales in Senegambia fell into two partly separate hierarchies, one for Europeans and other overseas recruits, the other for the Senegambians. The one ran from the Royal Governor (or the Director of a Company's affairs) down to the lowest foot soldier. The second ran through a variety of African and Afro-European servants and craftsmen down to the "castle slaves" or laptots belonging to the company or government, though some slaves and laptots were rented from their masters for short-term work. Samples of the two pay scales at various dates are given in tables A14.1 and A15.2.

The two different pay scales had a different structure. The African salaries, for example, had a range of minimum to maximum pay that varied from 1 to 3 up to 1 to 13, with a mean at 1 to 6. (Table A14.1.) Expatriate salaries, by contrast, ranged from 1 to 7 upwards to 1 to 202, with a mean at 1 to 76—about ten times the African mean. This difference can be taken as a sign that the fluid societies of the Afro-European trading communities were relatively egalitarian, compared either with Europe or with other societies in Senegambia. The European scale also reflected European society of the *ancien régime,* which was far from egalitarian.

Given the fact of European dominance in the trade enclaves, the two pay scales might be imagined as the two ends of a single hierarchy, with an area of overlap between the bottom of the European scale and the top of the African. In fact, the scales overlapped more than that. A man at the bottom rung of the European ladder was not markedly better off than one at the bottom rung of the African. The poorest European soldier might have slightly better pay than a hired laptot (who had to pay half his wages to his owner), but the laptot was more at home in the culture, more likely to be able to get something he wanted for his money, and far more likely to have disease immunities that allowed a reasonable life expectancy. From the employer's point of view, the officials sometimes calculated that it cost about the same to buy

an additional castle slave as it did to add and maintain a new
European soldier in the garrison.[1]

Comparisons of money wages are not very illuminating, though
they can be of some help. An able-bodied seaman in the French or
British slave trade in the late eighteenth or early nineteenth
century made an annual salary of about £24, plus keep.[2] This looks
like twice to four times the earnings of a Senegalese laptot or
Gambian "butler," but an annual wage of, say, £8 measured the
European value of the goods paid over to the Senegambian worker.
In fact, the real value was a good deal more once it had been
transferred into locally procured food, clothing, and shelter.
Curiously enough, the annual wage paid to a laptot (half of which
went to his master) was not far from the price of a trade slave
in either the early eighteenth or early nineteenth century (though
it was lower in a period like the 1780's, when slave prices reached
their peak). This should not be taken to imply, however, that the
rent of a slave was "one year's purchase," but only that an un-
skilled trade slave had a very low opportunity cost.

It is difficult to translate money wages into real wages, especially when the money wages were actually the European cost of goods
paid over to the staff, which the staff then sold to buy what they
wanted. In general, however, it appears that real wages probably increased slightly over time, as money wages certainly did by a facto
of 2 to 3.5. If millet is taken as an example, with the price in
1684-88 equal to 100, no later price was that low, and the "ordinary
price of the 1750's (admittedly a dry period) stood at index 270.
Scanty evidence (two price quotations only) shows it back down to 1
in the 1780's and 121 in 1831-35, though it was back to 203 in 1841
45.[3] Beef prices are often quoted as so much "per head," which is
not a helpful indicator of the amount of actual meat involved, but
the price apparently remained stable through most of the eighteenth
century and then rose by about 50 per cent in the early nineteenth.
Even these increases would be countered to some degree by the sharp
lower prices of European cloth in the early nineteenth century. (S
appendix 15 below.) It seems safe, however, to make an informed gu
that real wages rose by an unknown amount less than the rise in mon
wages.

SOURCES

1. "An estimate of Expenses . . . in the River Senegal and its
Dependencies for one year," n.d. (c. 1763), CO 267/12.

2. G. Martin, *Nantes au xviiie siècle: L'ère des négriers (1714
1774)* (Paris, 1931), p. 44; A. R. Onslow to Liverpool Customs House
13 November 1788, in written answer to the Board of Trade, Board of
Trade Report, part 2: L. Lacroix, *Les derniers négriers* (Paris,
1952), p. 149.

3. For the 1680's, T 70/546; memoir of 15 May 1754, ANF, C6 14;
Saugnier, *Voyages*, 1:306; for period after 1831, Gambia Blue Books,
T 90.

4. T 70/546; price tariff for 1740, ANF, C6 23; Saugnier, *Voyage*
1:306-7; Chenau, "Notes laissés," 26 August 1825, ANS, 13 G 164.

Table A14.1

Wages and Salaries Paid Senegambians by European Companies and Governments, 1685-1848

Annual receipts expressed in prime-cost equivalent by pounds sterling.
M indicates legal maximum wage.
Italics indicate payments by English, nonitalics by French.

Year	Place	Grommettas, foremen	Laptots, sailors, butlers (and keep)	Castle slaves, unskilled workers	Skilled craftsmen	Linguists	Riverboat captains	Ratio, min. to max.
1685[1]	Senegal	--	2.40	--	--	--	--	--
1719[2]	Senegal	--	3.40	--	--	--	--	--
1731[3]	Gambia	--	--	3.10	--	--	--	1T
1731[4]	Gambia	--	--	8.00	--	--	--	--
1763[5]	Senegal	--	--	30.00 (slave, cost plus year's keep and salary)	--	11.00	--	58
1766[6]	Gorée	--	6.10	4.60	11.30	9.80	22.70	1:13
1768[7]	Gorée	--	--	--	--	37.50	79.30	1:8
1781[8]	Gorée	--	5.00	--	--	--	12.50	1:4
1784[9]	Senegal	--	--	3.00	6.10	12.10	--	1:3
1780's[10]	Gambia	12.50	4.20	--	--	12.10	--	1:6
1786[11]	Senegal	--	6.60	--	--	10.50	42.00	1:7
1787[12]	Senegal	--	--	6.20	--	5.00	41.30	1:4
1802[13]	Senegal	--	--	--	--	--	--	1:4
1810[14]	Senegal	--	8.30	12.70 M	46.00 M	--	--	--
1826[15]	Gajaaga	16.20	4.70	5.80	37.50	--	--	1:8
1827[16]	Gambia	--	--	24.00	40.50	--	--	--
1828[17]	Senegal	21.30	--	5.60	--	16.40	--	1:3
1829[18]	Gajaaga	23.50	18.80	--	--	--	--	--
1833-34[20]	Senegal	23.30	14.10	--	--	23.30	--	--
1836[21]	Senegal	--	9.30	--	--	--	--	--
1843[22]	Senegal	17.40	11.60	--	--	--	34.80	1:3
1846[23]	Senegal	--	--	9.30	--	--	--	--
1847[24]	Senegal	--	--	17.50 M	--	--	--	--
1848[25]	Gambia	--	--	12.50	56.30	--	--	--
Mean ratio								1:6

Sources on page 85.

Table A14.2

Wages and Salaries Paid Expatriate Employees by European Companies and Governments in Senegambia, 1678-1809

In pound-sterling equivalents of goods paid, per year,* allowances included

Official	Gambia[26]* 1678	Gambia[4]	Senegal[27] 1736	Bambuhu[28] 1740	Ft. Lewis[5] 1763	Gorée[6] 1763-66	Gorée[7] 1768	St. Louis[9] 1784-87	St. Louis[29] 1809
Governor	--	250	96	239	200	378	317	605	1,188
Deputy Governor or Chief	--	150	64	--	100	--	--	269	
Merchant	--	150	64	--	100	--	--	269	
Secretary	--	100	--	--	80	--	--	--	
Surgeon	--	100	22	32	100	--	--	40	
Engineer	--	--	--	159	--	95	--	60	
Miner	--	--	--	16	--	--	--	--	
Chaplain	--	--	19	--	--	47	--	--	
Missionary	--	--	--	--	--	--	13	60	238
Factor	35	80	26	--	--	--	--	118	
Writer	--	60	16	24	60	--	--	81	71
Skilled tradesman (carpenter, mason, etc.)	--	50	19	20	23	113	114	22	
Chief military officer	--	--	--	239	--	56	57	134	71
Lieutenant	--	--	--	28	--	95	95	71	143
Captain	--	--	--	119	--	6	11	111	29
Sergeant	--	--	6	9	40	--	6	12	9
Private soldier	--	17	3	4	30	--	--	3	
Ratio of min. to max. by columns	--	1:15	1:32	1:60	1:7	1:63	1:53	1:202	1:132

Mean ratio, min. to max., 1:71

Sources for appendix 14 tables:

1. La Courbe, *Premier voyage*, p. 18.
2. Brué to Violaine, 23 October 1719, BN, FF, NA, 9341.
3. Gambia Accounts, 1731, T 70/558, f. 107.
4. T 70/168, f. 102.
5. "An Estimate of Expenses . . in the River Senegal and its Dependencies for one year," undated, but c. 1763, CO 267/12. A return for 1765 in CO 388/52 varies only in carrying privates at £25, sergeants at £70, and clerks at £50.
6. Mesnager, "Etat, des appointments paiés . . . colonie de Gorée," 1766, ANF, C6 15; Shefer, *Instructions générales*, 1:14-15.
7. "Etat des dépenses à faire à Gorée pendant l'anée 1768," ANF, C6 15.
8. Pay list dated 1 June 1781, CO 267/7 (Gorée under English occupation).
9. "Dépenses général, 1784," ANF, C6 18, Durand, *Sénégal*, 1:365.
10. Evidence of Captain Heatley, Board of Trade Report, part 1.
11. "Etat général de la dépense du Bateau *le Bienfaisant*," 29 May 1786, ANF, C6 19.
12. Durand, *Sénégal*, 2:365.
13. J. Monteilhet, "Les finances et commerce du Sénégal pendant les guerres de la Revolution et de l'Empire," *CEHSAOF*, 2:362-412 (1917), p. 43.
14. Maxwell, replies to H.M. Commissioners, 1 January 1811, CO 267/29.
15. Arrêté no. 7, 4 March 1826, *Bulletin administratif*, 1:125-26, a schedule of wages to be paid by the government.
16. J. Rowan, Report of 9 June 1827, CO 267/93, p. 7.
17. Agricultural wages. Perrottet, report for 1825-28, ANF-OM, Sénégal XIII 17.
18. Duranton to Governor, 7 August 1828, ANS, 1 G 8.
19. Arrêté no. 22, 3 December 1829, *Bulletin administratif*, 1:271-72.
20. "Extrait du mémoire de l'ordonnateur sur son service de 1833 et 1834," ANF-OM, Sénégal XIII 17.
21. Guillet, "Notes de l'ordonnateur sur l'affranchissement des captifs," 20 January 1836, ANS, K 7.
22. Arrêté no. 57, 10 June 1843, *Bulletin administratif*, 2:70-71.
23. Agricultural labor. Delanvire to Governor, 22 July 1846, ANF-OM, Sénégal XIII 17.
24. Arrêté no. 22, 1 March 1847, *Bulletin administratif*, 4:23-26.
25. Blue Book, 1848, p. 160, CO 90/22.
26. T. Thurloe to RAC, Gambia, 28 March 1678, T 70/10.
27. Delcourt, *La France au Sénégal*, pp. 400-440.
28. Unsigned planning memoir for a mining establishment in Bambuhu, ANF, C6 23.
29. C. M. C. Picard, "Des possessions françaises en Afrique" (unpublished mss., Paris, 1814), in ANF, C6 28.

15 | THE CALCULATION OF IMPORTS, EXPORTS, AND TERMS OF TRADE

The Gambian accounts of the Royal African Company for the years 1683-88 are preserved in the Public Record Office, London, as T 70/546. Among other things, they include a copy of the invoice of each cargo received at James Fort over the six-year period, indicating for each commodity in the shipment the prime cost in Europe plus any additional costs for packing or the like. These prices are thus effectively f.o.b. some European port, usually London.

The total of forty-four cargoes listed can be treated as a sample of Gambian imports generally at this period. When the goods intended for the upkeep of the fort are excluded, along with imports of minor importance and those with inadequate data for comparison with later periods, the result is a 74-per-cent sample of the total, incidentally including all commodities that were 5 per cent or more of the total. This sample forms the basis of the 1683-88 data in tables 6.6, 8.1, and others derived from them.

The export invoices are not shown in the Gambian accounts, nor are all transactions for the purchase of export commodities. But about 25 per cent of all transactions were recorded. These transactions covered the purchase of provisions and other Gambian products for the use of the forts, as well as exports. The sample can therefore be used as a guide for estimating exports. Assuming that the cargoes arriving each year were spent for goods in that year, and that total purchases went to the various export commodities in the same proportion as in the recorded sample of purchases, it is possible to calculate the amount probably spent for each commodity. These transactions are recorded as payments in bars, which need translation into £ sterling values. Since the invoices of imports give sterling prices and itemize the goods imported, it is possible to calculate the total £/bar ratio for each year (see table 6.6), and that ratio can be applied to any payment in bars to obtain a value in sterling. With that information, it is possible to divide the recorded sample of purchases into the percentage spent for each exported commodity and the percentage spent

for provisions—either for the post or for storing slave ships.
It would be a reasonable inference to take these percentages,
apply them to the total value of the imported cargoes, and take
the result as estimated exports—if it were not for the fact that
no allowance would then be made for the European goods imported
for use at the forts. It is difficult, in fact, to make this allowance with extreme accuracy. An item like cordage was obviously
for Gambia river shipping, but gunpowder might have been for use
or for sale to Africans. An allowance can be made within broad
limits, however. The import sample consisting of all major items
usually sold (including gunpowder) comes to 73.5 per cent of total
imports. Given the fact that many items were omitted because they
were individually insignificant, though clearly for sale rather
than for use by the forts, the imports for the use of the forts
could not have exceeded 20 per cent of the total, and were probably much less. Where these data have been used in calculations,
therefore, as in appendix 11 and table 4.5, the estimated exports
have been arbitrarily reduced by 10 per cent to take account of
this source of error.

IMPORTS OF THE EIGHTEENTH CENTURY

The European records were almost always more complete for the
goods they carried away than for those they left in return. The
surviving documents contain frequent, if incomplete, lists of
prices paid in Europe and prices on the coast in bars or other
local currencies. Travelers often listed the import commodities
that sold most easily, presumably for the guidance of those who
might follow in the African trade. The missing data are the
quantities sold, which have to be reconstructed by indirect means
for all periods before the beginning of regular customs house
records in the 1820's and 1830's. After many and time-consuming
attempts to construct some approximation of the gross barter terms
of trade (based on quantity changes, as opposed to the net barter
terms of trade based on changing prices), I have had to admit defeat—though with a continued suspicion that it may be possible
for a more ingenious manipulator of rare and inaccurate data to
succeed in future.

The sources of Senegambian import data in the eighteenth century
are essentially of two kinds. Several officials of the Compagnie
des Indes or the French government prepared statements that pro-
jected their needs over the next year or so. The three samples
that lie behind the first three columns in table A15.1 are somewhat different from one another. The first is a projection of
future needs on an annual basis, where the commodities are listed
by quantity, price in Europe, and region of consumption in Senegambia. The second is simply a list of commodities needed for
the next year, and it may be biased by the fact that the forts
could well have been overstocked in some goods and not in others.
The third is a similar order for goods, but for three consecutive
years, so that the annual averages help to iron out the possible
overstocking error. The lists for column 3 had another deficiency

Table A15.1

Major Senegambian Imports by Way of the French Trade Enclave at Selected Dates, 1718-1850, in Percentages

Commodity	(1) 1718	(2) 1745	(3) 1752-54	(4) 1786-87	(5) 1836-40	(6) 1846-50
Metals, metalware	29.2	43.3	33.8	(See source note)	0.4	1.8
Iron	8.5	11.3	14.3		28.2	24.3
Silver	13.2	32.0	19.5		47.4	36.8
Other	7.5	---	---			
Textiles, clothing	24.0	39.0	38.0	77.3	75.6	61.1
European origin	24.0	2.0	11.7	24.9	28.2	24.3
Indian origin		37.0	26.3	52.4	47.4	36.8
Arms, ammunition	5.3	5.2	6.4	3.5	3.7	6.8
Beads, semiprecious stones	34.0	5.0	12.9	---	---	4.4
Food, spices	1.2	0.1	0.4	---	---	---
Paper	1.8	1.4	0.9	---	---	---
Cowries	1.0	---	---	7.1	---	---
Miscellaneous consumables	3.6	5.9	7.7	12.1	13.3	25.9
Spirits	3.6	5.9	7.7	8.1	4.3	5.2
Wine	---	---	---	4.0	2.1	8.4
Tobacco	---	---	---	---	6.9	12.3
Total	100.0	100.0	100.0	100.0	100.0	100.0

Sources:
Col. 1, from table 8.2.
Col. 2, Major imports selected from "État des marchandises, vivres, et utenciles nécessaires pour le commerce et l'entretien de la concession du Sénégal pendant l' année 1745 . . .," ANF, C6 12. Prices supplied at prime cost for nearest date available. Data in this and column 3 judged to be not very reliable, though areas of agreement between them support common assessments.
Col. 3, quantities recorded for three years in annual orders for merchandise from France (ANF, C6 14), combined with prices as of 1763-64 recorded in Gaignet de Laulnais, Guide de commerce, p. 312, and Demanet, Nouvelle histoire, 1:251-54. The data in this column judged to be not very reliable.
Col. 4, major imports selected from a return of French exports to Africa for these two years in ANF, C6 19; sample comes to about 72 per cent of total. Metals were aggregated with naval stores, thus no data for this category.
Cols. 5 and 6, major imports selected from annual returns in Statistiques coloniales. Categories judged major came to about 70 per cent of all imports.

88

in that silver was no longer counted as a commodity, though it
was still imported in large quantities. Fortunately, this could
be corrected by reference to other estimates of silver imports at
this period.[1] The data for columns 2 and 3 alike listed only
quantities, not prices. These had to be supplied from a variety
of contemporary evidence,[2] and a certain amount of sheer guess-
work was required, though the prices of the more important commodities could be established as indicated for table A15.3.

In spite of the inevitably high level of probable error in the
first three columns of table A15.1, they clearly partake of a
similar pattern of demand and one that makes a sharp contrast
with the new pattern of demand that was to emerge in the early
nineteenth century (columns 5 and 6). The second half of the
eighteenth century lies between the end of the French company in
1758 and the new phase of nineteenth-century Senegalese government record-keeping. Column 4 represents French exports to West
Africa in 1786-87. Its only value is to suggest possible timing
of the transition between the early eighteenth and the early
nineteenth centuries.

The second source of import data in the first half of the
eighteenth century is the surviving account books of the Royal
African Company. The series that was so valuable for the 1680's
is only partial for the early decades of the century, but a regular series begins again in 1727 through 1741. This time, however,
the invoices of consignments were not included, though individual
transactions with Africans are reported in greater detail. These
records were used in chapter 6 to provide a quantitative basis
for discussing differences between prime costs and bar prices.
Some of the key transactions reported there occurred at either
end of the decade of the 1730's, and the mean of nine large transactions for slaves in 1731 and 1740-41 is taken as a representative sample of the goods the British were importing into the
Gambia at that period. But the record thus established simply
gives the proportions of an unknown total. It seems to make
sense in comparison with the more accurate figures for a half-
century earlier and a half-century later, but data presented in
three significant figures should not be taken as a claim to
that degree of accuracy. (Table A15.2, column 2.)

In spite of the underlying problems with all of these data, they
are probably accurate enough to provide a basis for estimating
the changing import proportions for Senegambia over the whole
period—in effect, a guide to the makeup of the changing bundle
of goods the Senegambians were buying from Europe. Since the
data are most nearly adequate at approximate fifty-year intervals,
in the 1680's, 1730's, and so on, estimates can be found for these
decades. The decade of the 1680's depends on the RAC pattern of
imports for 1683-88, for lack of French information. In the
1730's, both French and English imports can be taken into account.
The closest Senegalese sample is that of 1745 (table A15.1), while
estimates for the Gambia are available for the 1730's (table A15.2).
The relative importance of French and British carriers of imports
is not known, but it can be assumed that their import business
would have been roughly proportional to the exports each carried—

Table A15.2

Samples of the Distribution of Gambian Imports, 1680-1850, in Percentages

Commodity	(1) 1684-88	(2) 1731-41	(3) 1831-40	(4) 1841-50
Metals, metalware	33.7	34.6	5.1	8.1
Iron bars	24.9	8.2	4.2	3.5
Silver	4.2	16.3	---	---
Copper	1.0	.8	---	---
Brassware	1.7	7.6	---	---
Pewterware	1.9	1.7	---	---
Hardware	---	---	0.9	4.6
Woolen cloth	1.4	3.1		
Red cloth	1.4	3.1		
Indian textiles	1.6	7.5	19.7	36.9
Long cloths	---	5.2		
Bafts	1.6	2.3		
Tapseals				
Other textiles	1.0	11.2		
Silesias	1.0	4.4		
Fringe	---	5.4		
Manchester cloth	---	1.4		
Cutlery, weapons	8.1	13.8	28.8	21.4
Firearms	1.5	8.9	15.8	13.7
Gunpowder	1.2	4.9	13.0	7.7
Knives	---	---	---	---
Swords	5.4	---	---	---
Beads, semiprecious stones	39.9	25.7	15.5	8.5
Glass beads	13.9	11.3	8.2	5.4
Coral, amber	18.4	1.9	7.3	3.1
Crystal	7.6	8.5	---	---
Carnelians	---	4.0	---	---
Miscellaneous consumables	14.1	4.2	30.8	24.9
Spirits	14.1	4.2	7.3	8.1
Wine	---	---	2.9	3.1
Tobacco	---	---	20.6	13.7
Totals	100.0	100.0	100.0	100.0

Sources: Col. 1, table 8.1. Col. 2, the mean of six sample transactions for slaves in Sept.-Dec. 1731 (T 70/558) and three transactions for slaves in June 1740 and 1741 (T 70/573 and 575). Cols. 3 and 4, based on selected major exports from Gambia Blue Books, annual, CO 90. Major exports included in sample were approximately 88 per cent of total.

62.8 per cent for the English to 37.2 per cent for the French,
following table A15.6. The two samples are therefore weighted
accordingly to arrive at the estimate in table A15.3.

Even though it is not possible to follow the full picture of
changing quantities, prices, and values of each commodity imported, a few selected commodities can be followed. Fortunately,
some of these were the most important and the most uniform over
time. A fairly reliable sample of prices and quantities can be
taken from the administrative report of 1718, listing future
needs (see table 8.2 above), and the sample of 1752-54 provides
another point of contact forty-five years later. The data in
table A15.3 are thus raw material for tracing changes in quantities and prices over an extended period of time.

NINETEENTH-CENTURY IMPORTS

The Europeans returned to the two river mouths and to Gorée in
a new age of government statistics; most of the old problems of
sampling and the like disappear. In their place come new problems
of interpreting the governments' numbers. One of the most significant is that of understanding the aggregated total imports
or total exports. Two sources of records are often available:
first, the records of the metropolitan ports, showing exports to
and imports from the Gambia or Senegal; second, the records of
the colonial customs service, which should show the whole of
foreign trade, not just its metropolitan branch. Even if allowance is made for such nonmetropolitan trade, the two records
rarely correspond well.

A more severe problem appears with the different ways of reporting foreign trade flows. One possibility was to treat the
colonial enclave as an entrepôt, so that everything entering or
leaving a town like Bathurst was counted as part of foreign trade,
even if it only went across the Gambia to Ñomi. A second method
can be called "colonial reporting," after the mentality that gave
rise to it. Instead of treating the European posts as entrepôts,
the customs officials acted as though the enclaves were seaports
of a territorial unit embracing the whole hinterland. Thus an
export was counted only when it was shipped outward bound by sea,
and an import was counted only when it arrived by sea. In spite
of its arrogance, the "colonial" method of customs reporting is
much the most satisfactory. With the coming and going of hundreds
of local small craft, entrepôt reporting of substantial accuracy
was simply not possible, though an ocean-going ship could hardly
escape notice; and the colonial method has the further advantage
of treating the hinterland as an economic region, rather than
simply trying to measure the flow of trade in either direction
through the ports.

Furthermore, the customs services themselves were not always
careful about clearly following one system or the other. Table
A15.4, however, reproduces the official annual totals, indicating
the form of reporting. Only the years 1832-35 can be interpreted
as a genuine attempt to measure the flow of imports into Senegambia—whether accurate or not is another matter. If the reporting

Table A15.3

Imports of Selected Commodities in 1718 and 1753 by Price and Quantity

Commodity and unit	Quantity 1718	Quantity 1752	European Price per unit, £ sterling 1718	1752	Annual value imported 1718	1752
Silver coins or pataques[a] (no.)	18,850	14,000	£0.2048	£0.2089	£3,860	£2,924
Guns[b] (no.)	224	1,784	2.56	.342	625	610
Sabers (no.)	550	933	.307	.189[c]	169	176
Gunpowder (kgms)	1,028	2,448	.209	.05278[d]	215	129
Brandy (ltrs)	13,876	55,878	.165	.0278[e]	2,288	1,161
Iron bars (no.)	6,055	11,333	.307	.189[f]	1,860	2,142
Paper (reams)	600	567	.510	.250[f]	307	49
Lead (kgms)	1,566	3,019	.552[d]	.0068[d]	86	12
Bafatas or *toiles noires*[g] (pieces)	1,476	5,000	1.20	.788[f]	1,770	3,940
Silesias (pieces)	2,500	367	.666	.189	1,664	69

Sources: Data for 1718, "Mémoire général sur le commerce du Sénégal," ANF, C6 14; data for 1752, "Etats général des marchandises nécessaires à la concession du Sénégal, pour les années 1752, 1753, et 1754," ANF, C6 12.

Notes:

a. The pataques in use shifted from the 50-stuiver rix-dollar in 1718 to the 28-stuiver coin after the 1730's. Price for 1718 is as given, but the 1752 price is simply an adjustment to account for the change in average exchange value between Dutch and English dollar in Amsterdam as reported by Posthumus, *Prices in Holland*, pp. 590 ff. Quantity shown in 1752 is as though measured in rix-dollars.

b. Guns ordered in 1718 were relatively high priced "buccaneer" guns, while later report dealt mainly with trade guns. The price of trade guns would not have changed so much over this period. Gun price for 1754 is the English price reported in "Account of a Large Cargo," 9 October 1754, T 70/1518.

c. Price is that of 1763 from Gaignat de Lauinais, *Guide de commerce*, p. 312.

d. Annual average Amsterdam price quoted in Posthumus, *Prices in Holland*.

e. Annual average price of French brandy in Amsterdam, 1752-54, Posthumus, *Prices in Holland*.

f. Price from Fuuta customs list, 1757, ANF, C6 14.

g. For 1718, "bafatas" at £1.43 the P. are combined with "toiles bleues" at £1.088. Both were about 16 meters long and apparently predecessors of, if not nearly identical with, the cloths later called *pièces de Guinée*. In the 1750's they appear as "toiles noires," of nearly the same size.

Table A15.4
Official Statistics of Senegambian Imports

a. Imports of French goods from France, classified as "commerce spécial."
b. Imports of European products only, disregarding imports from the hinterland destined for re-export overseas.
c. Imports from France, including French re-exports of other origin, classified as "commerce général."
d. Entrepôt reporting, including at least some African products imported for ultimate re-export.

Year	Senegal & dependencies (1,000 fr)	£ equivalent	Gambia (£ sterling)	Total
1818	2,551[a]	105,356		
1819	1,842[a]	78,469		
1820	1,624[a]	62,362		
1821	1,594[a]	61,210		
1822	866[a]	33,601	45,440[b]	
1823	1,886[b]	72,422		
1824	2,257[b]	87,797		
1825	3,948[c]	150,814		
1826	4,065[c]	156,909		
1827	4,717[c]	183,491		
1828	3,973[c]	155,344	50,269[b]	205,613
1829	4,551[c]	178,399	43,081[b]	221,480
1830	4,121[c]	158,659	32,527[b]	191,186
1831	3,094[c]	121,285	39,255[b]	160,540
1832	3,369[b]	129,707	50,522[b]	180,229
1833	3,885[b]	150,350	37,702[b]	188,052
1834	4,009[b]	156,351	63,455[b]	219,806
1835	5,312[b]	206,106	75,502[d]	281,608
1836	6,962[b]	270,126	114,772[d]	384,898
1837	10,205[b]	395,954	99,763[d]	495,717
1838	13,378[d]	519,066	105,625[d]	624,691
1839	10,230[d]	401,016	153,903[d]	554,919
1840	11,262[d]	440,344	105,397[d]	545,741
1841	10,331[d]	402,909	73,670[d]	476,579
1842	6,799[d]	263,801	114,063[d]	377,864

Year	St. Louis	Gorée	£ equivalent	Gambia (£ sterling)	Total
1843	6,290[d]	3,053[d]	361,574	107,018[d]	468,592
1844	6,110[d]	3,357[d]	367,320	96,106[d]	463,426
1845	8,540[d]	3,066[d]	447,992	117,890[d]	565,882
1846	10,368[d]	2,806[d]	508,516	94,175[d]	602,691
1847	8,728[d]	3,163[d]	461,371	90,521[d]	551,892
1848	4,762[d]	3,062[d]	301,224	68,719[d]	369,943
1849	5,412[d]	2,595[d]	316,277	73,410[d]	389,687
1850	5,090[d]	2,752[d]	308,975	86,036[d]	395,011

Sources: Senegal and dependencies: 1817-18, ANF-OM, Sénégal XIII 72; 1819-23 and 1825-31, J. P. Duchon-Doris, Jr., *Commerce des toiles bleues, dit Guinées* (Paris, 1842), p. 64; 1832 onward, *Statistiques coloniales,* annual volumes. Gambia: 1823, CO 267/93, f. 9; 1828 onward, Gambia Blue Books, annual series, CO 90.

for the years after 1835 were more accurate, it might be possible
to manipulate the data to arrive at an approximation of colonial
reporting; but the habits of colonial reporting in the Senegalese
and Gambian customs service appear to have carried over into the
period of entrepôt reporting in the late 1830's and afterwards.
(Export statistics are more susceptible to correction [see below,
p. 95].) The total annual imports are therefore printed
simply because they are official, not because they are likely
to be accurate.

The total figures, however, are more inaccurate in respect to
local movements of African products than they are in respect to
the major imports from Europe. It is therefore possible to use
the official trade figures appearing in the *Statistiques coloniales* to follow the further movement of the major import items
already traced through parts of the eighteenth century. In this
respect, the annual average values and quantities reported by
the Senegalese customs house appear to be accurate enough. The
only problem of incommensurates is with iron, which was reported
as so many bars in the eighteenth century but now appears as so
many tons. If, however, the value reported for 1752-54 is divided
by the average Amsterdam price for Swedish bar iron, the total of
6,055 bars each year appears to have been about 107.8 metric
tons—yielding a weight per bar of 17.8 kgs, clearly the old standard bar size of the 1680's. It can be assumed that the Company
was using the same size bar in 1718 as well.

Silver was still treated as money, not a commodity, in the nineteenth century. It therefore remained off the import lists.
Statistiques coloniales for 1839, however, carried a note (p. 90)
to the effect that silver coins valued at 92,068 francs had been
imported during the year. Since this amounted to some 3.9 per
cent of annual average imports for that period, it was a significant amount. Even though data for other years is missing, it is
better to enter silver (even on the basis of a single year) than
to leave it out altogether.

EXPORTS IN THE EIGHTEENTH AND EARLY NINETEENTH CENTURIES

It is possible to document Senegambian exports in some detail
for most of the eighteenth century. The available record of
quantities exported in each of the major products other than
slaves is found in appendix 11, and various estimates of the
export slave trade are found in chapter 8.

As with imports, the best eighteenth-century aggregated record
is that left by the Compagnie des Indes, while the best microcos-
mic record of individual transactions is found in the account books
of the Royal African Company. But the RAC paid little attention
to the totals exported, because it no longer had a monopoly or
even a claim to one. The French records and estimates for their
share of the trade alone, however, are assembled in table 15.5
to show the possible levels of their trade at various dates.
These data are useful for some purposes, but they have to be interpreted with care. The French sources of supply within

Senegambia were normally those to the north, hence higher in gum, lower in wax, and lower in hides than the Gambian sources. Slaves and gold were variable, depending upon whether the Senegal or Gambia route was more successful at the moment. They cannot, therefore, be taken as a representative sample of Senegambia as a whole.

Estimates that attempt to show the picture of exports for the whole region are perhaps less accurate, but they are more meaningful; and the really significant shifts are so large that a low degree of accuracy can still show the main trends. Estimates and accounts that are designed to measure the approximate flow of Senegambian exports at half-century intervals are included in table A15.6.

With the better records kept by colonial governments in the late 1820's and early 1830's, the problem of entrepôt as opposed to colonial customs reporting recurs. The official government statistics are reproduced in table A15.7 with indication of the form of reporting that lay behind them. In contrast to the import statistics from the same sources, however, these data can be manipulated into a more meaningful form. The French form of reporting makes it possible to exclude re-exports bound toward the hinterland. This has been done in A15.7 so as to preserve colonial reporting from 1832 onward—in effect, reporting the exports of the whole hinterland. For the Gambia, however, the government shifted to entrepôt reporting after 1835. This can be adjusted, however, by separating out the major exports that certainly went overseas for each year from 1832 onward to 1850. The crucial list of peanuts and peanut products, gum, gold, hides, ivory, mahogany, and wax totalled 86 per cent of all exports in 1832-34, the last years of colonial reporting. Assuming that the sum of these major exports would continue to be about 86 per cent of the total, it is possible to add their values each year and increase the total accordingly to arrive at an overall estimate. The result is far from perfect, but it is at least more accurate than the official figures, and it makes possible a set of commensurate export estimates for the whole of Senegambia over the years 1832-50-as shown in table A15.8.

The remaining problem is to trace the major exports into the nineteenth century, which is comparatively simple, though some uncertainties remain on account of differing prices reported by the two customs services. The accuracy is nevertheless enough to measure the gross changes that took place over the half-century before the 1830's.

AN IMPORT PRICE INDEX, 1671-1704

The main data problem for calculating levels of trade (beyond those encountered in the examination of imports and exports separately) is that of finding long runs of prices. Gross barter terms of trade cannot be calculated in any case, for lack of sufficient information on volume of import trade, and this obviously rules out income terms of trade as well. Net barter terms of

Table A15.5

Estimates and Returns of Exports from Senegambia by the Compagnie des Indes and Other French Shippers in Selected Years, 1687 to 1824-26 (metric quantities, values not f.o.b. but usually price paid the African supplier at an Atlantic port)

Year		Gold	Gum	Hides	Ivory	Slaves	Wax	Total
1687	Quantity	1.71 kg	200 tons	30,000	15 tons	500	5 tons	
	Value	£115	£914	£915	£540	£1,700	£634	£4,818
	% of total	2.4	19.0	19.0	11.2	35.3	13.2	100.0
1693	Quantity	2.94 kg	294 tons	33,500	35 tons	900	20 tons	
	Value	£197	£1,342	£624	£665	£2,016	£597	£5,441
	% of total	3.6	24.7	11.5	12.2	37.1	11.0	100.0
1718	Quantity	12.24 kg	2,200 tons	6,800	24 tons	1,986	23 tons	
	Value	£655	£2,723	£205	£1,537	£10,445	£1,507	£17,072
	% of total	3.8	15.9	1.2	9.0	61.2	8.8	100.0
1723	Quantity	12.20 kg	392 tons	10,000	20 tons	2,000	49 tons	
	Value	£1,139	£2,136	£223	£1,282	£10,680	£2,848	£18,308
	% of total	6.2	11.7	1.2	7.0	58.3	15.6	100.0
1733	Quantity	24.50 kg	49 tons	---	5 tons	1,200	10 tons	
	Value	£1,640	£131	---	£157	£4,248	£570	£6,746
	% of total	24.3	1.9	---	2.3	63.0	8.4	100.0
1740	Quantity	25.9 kg	387 tons	569	300 kg	1,481	---	
	Value	£1,606	£2,345	£1	£15	£13,433	---	£17,400
	% of total	9.2	13.5	---	---	77.2	---	100.0
1750	Quantity	55.1 kg	1,028 tons	---	8 tons	1,750	4 tons	
	Value	£2,689	£3,557	---	£164	£25,200	£102	£31,712
	% of total	8.5	11.2	---	0.5	79.5	0.3	100.0
1784	Quantity	2.0 kg	339 tons	---	3 tons	1,071	---	
	Value	£178	£15,135	---	£364	£23,391	---	£39,068
	% of total	0.5	38.7	---	0.9	59.9	---	100.0
1786-88	Annual av. quantity	---	315 tons	493	6 tons	1,798	---	
	Value	---	£9,533	£9	£76	£49,481	---	£59,099
	% of total	---	16.1	---	0.1	83.7	---	100.0
1793-97	Annual av. quantity	---	316 tons	341	4 tons	---	---	
	Value	---	£9,594	£6	£51	---	---	£9,651
	% of total	---	99.4	0.1	0.5	---	---	100.0

					Total
1802–3					
Quantity	952 tons	795	1 ton	456	---
Value	£57,082	£15	£18	£12,549	£69,664
% of total	81.9	0.02	0.03	18.0	100.0
1822					
Quantity (St. Louis only)	754 tons	16,829	2 tons	8 tons	---
Value	£50,518	£2,104	£444	£1,205	£54,271
% of total	93.1	3.9	0.8	2.2	100.0
1824–26					
Annual av. quantity (St. Louis only)	1,034 tons	26,000	8 tons	20 tons	---
Value	£71,346	£4,713	£2,425	£1,958	£80,442
% of total	88.7	5.9	3.0	2.4	100.0

Sources: 1687, Table A15.6. 1693, La Courbe, "Mémoire sur le commerce de Guinée," ANF, C6 2, also printed in the Introduction by P. Cultru to LaCourbe, *Premier voyage*, pp. li–lii. Quantities are expectation, not experience. Prices are based on bar prices, therefore not very accurate. 1718, unsigned, "Mémoire général sur le commerce du Sénégal," ANF, C6 14. Quantities are expectation, not experience. Prices are based on bar prices. 1723, unsigned, "Mémoire sur le commerce du Sénégal," 11 October 1723, ANF, C6 7. Quantities are expectation, values are based on bar prices. 1733, Levens, Memorandum of 16 August 1733, ANF, C6 10, for quantities, with prices drawn from 1723 data above, though prices closer in time were used when available. 1740, Unsigned, "Etat de la dépense général de la concession du 1ère juin 1738 au 31e mai 1740," ANF, C6 12. Data extracted are the annual average for the two-year period, working with bar prices indicated in the document. 1750, the mean of estimated range of exports by M. Adanson, "Pièces instructives concernant l'isle de Gorée," ANF, C6 15. Also printed in Machat, *Documents*, p. 80. Values supplied for closest possible date. 1784, actual measure of quantity and value exported, from Labarthe, *Voyage en Sénégal*, pp. 103–4. 1786–88, actual measurement of exports from Gorée and Saint Louis, annual averages at annual prices or closest available. ANF, C6 19. 1793–97. Returns for year II through year VII of the revolutionary calendar (Sept. 22, 1793–Sept. 21, 1798), from "Renseignements sur le Sénégal," 1801, ANF, C6 27, pp. 225–26. 1802–3, returns for the last six months of the year X and the first six months of the year XI of the revolutionary calendar (March 1802–March 1803), in ANF C6 20. These figures are exceptional, since they fall largely within the period of the Peace of Amiens, when safe ocean shipping was possible, so that part of the totals represent a backlog from wartime years. Values are mainly those for the prewar years and are therefore not very reliable. 1822, "Situation de la Place de Saint Louis," 31 December 1822, ANF-OM, Sénégal XIII, 72, with prices added from other sources. 1824–26, annual average of statistical summaries for each year in ANS, 22 G 3. Prices are from other sources.

Table A15.6

Principal Senegambian Exports, Annual Averages at Half-Century Intervals

Commodity	St. Louis and Petite Côte	Gambia, including French-carried	Total exports	Unit value in sterling prime-cost equivalent	Total value	% share in total export
			The 1680's			
Gold (kgs)[1]	1.71	6.65	8.36	£67.00[2]	£ 560	5.0
Gum (tons)[3]	200	--	200	4.57	914	8.1
Hides (no.)[4]	30,000	11,200	43,200	.0305	952	8.5
Ivory (tons)[5]	15	23.7	38.7	36.00	1,393	12.4
Slaves (no.)[6]	500	1,330	1,830	3.40	6,222	55.3
Wax (tons)[7]	5	23.7	28.7	42.28	1,213	10.8
Total					£11,254	100.0
			The 1730's			
	Exported by French	English				
Gold (kgs)	24.18	5.0[9]	29.1	72.85	£ 2,120	7.8
Gum (tons)	4218	--	421	6.06[12]	2,551	9.4
Hides (no.)	569[13]	--	569	0.018[14]	10	--
Ivory (tons)	0.31[8]	25.4	25.7[15]	42.75[16]	1,099	4.0
Slaves (no.)	975[17]	2,140[5]	3,115	5,6216,10	17,506	64.3
Wax (tons)	1141[5]	11[15]	124	31.75[16]	3,937	14.5
Total					£27,223	100.0
			The 1780's[18]			
	Exported by French[18]	English[19]				
Gold (kgs)	2.1	--	2.1	£89.95[18]	£ 189	0.2
Gum (tons)	321	--	321	30.36[19]	9,746	12.0
Hides (no.)	493	--	493	.0191[19]	9	--
Ivory (tons)	5.3	9.1	14.4	13.77	198	0.2
Slaves (no.)	1,616	1,050	2,666	26.37[20]	70,302	86.5
Wax (tons)	--	30	30	29.00[21]	870	1.1
Total					£81,314	100.0

1. Quantity estimates are those of Ducasse, "Mémoire ou relation du S. du Casse sur son voyage de Guinée," ANF-OM, DFC Sénégal 1, no. 4.

2. Nearest local price is that reported by Labat for the end of the century, a prime-cost value of £34.84 in Gajaaga and £66.94 in Saint Louis. European value at the time was approximately fil4 per kg. (Labat, *Nouvelle relation*, 4:319.)

3. Estimates of gum exports differed, with Ducasse estimating 49 metric tons in 1687 while Chambonneau guessed 773 the next year. (Chambonneau to Marquis de Signilay, June 1688, ANF, C6 1.) Figure selected is based on these and on La Courbe, "Mémoire sur le commerce de Guinée," 1693, ANF, C6 2, who put it at about 196 tons. The price also follows La Courbe's indication in *Premier voyage*, pp. li-liii.

4. Estimate from Ducasse is 10,000 for the Senegal River and 20,000 for the Petite Côte (perhaps including some from the Gambia), and this is confirmed by Francisco de Lemos Coelho, who put the French exports at 35,000 to 40,000 in about 1680. (*Duas descriçoes seisentistas da Guiné de Francisco de Lemos Coelho*, ed. Damiao Peres [Lisbon, 1953].) Gambia figure is annual average exported by Royal African Company 1683-88, calculated from data in T 70/546, as indicated above, p. 86.

5. Quantity estimate for Senegal and the Petite Côte is that of Ducasse, while the Gambia figure is the annual average of RAC exports 1683-88 (T70/546). Price estimate is very uncertain, since large large tusks sold for about £48 while small ones brought only £24 per metric ton; £36 is simply the middle of this range.

6. Annual average purchase by RAC on the Gambia was 1,200 in 1683-88 (table 4.5). While French exports are more uncertain in number, the Gambia figure is increased to allow 10 per cent to the French. Estimates by contemporaneous observers are often based on the capacity as demonstrated by a recent "good year," rather than on a statistical average of good years and bad. The total figure adopted is the mean of T. Thurloe to RAC, 14 March 1677-68, printed in E. Donnan, *Documents Illustrative of the History of the Slave Trade to America*, 4 vols. (Washington, D. C., 1930-35), 1:234; Ducasse, "Mémoire ou relation du Sr. Ducasse sur son voyage de Guynée avec *La Tempeste* en 1687 et 1688," in Paul Roussier, *L'établissement d'Issiny, 1687-1702* (Paris, 1935), and La Courbe, "Mémoire sur le commerce du Sénégal, ANF, C6 2. Price is calculated from RAC performance 1683-88, T 70/546, as in table A8.1. It is *not* f.o.b. but is the price paid by the RAC, to preserve comparability to other prices.

7. Wax quantity estimates follow Ducasse in allowing 5 tons per year from the Petite Côte, a French export of 10 tons from the Gambia, plus the RAC annual average of 13.7 tons in 1683-88. Price is the annual average paid by the RAC in that period (T 70/546).

8. From appendix 11, average of data for period 1731-40, counting 1740 data twice, since these are two-year annual averages.

9. RAC accounts show transactions for gold in at least half of the years of this decade, but no total exports. This figure is an arbitrary guess.

10. French government subsidies of £2.53 per kg of gold and £0.52 per slave exported are not included.

11. Undated tariff of C1, c.1740, ANF, C6 23. All prices in this table are the prices normally paid to African suppliers in the port towns, not f.o.b. prices.

12. "Mémoire sur le prix de gomme," 1739, ANF, C6 8.

13. "Etat des dépenses général," 1 June 1738 to 31 May 1740, ANF, C6 12, annual average of the two-year period.

14. T 70/559, 1732 price from the calculated prime-cost of an assortment paid for hides. Conventional bar price of hides was equivalent to £0.0175 each.

15. "Mémoire concernant le commerce," enclosed with Commander Gorée to Director Saint Louis, 4 July 1741, ANF, C6 12. Estimates of English trade based on information from Albreda.

16. Annual average for 1732-41, see table 4.2.

17. Annual average of samples each year from Gambia Accounts, T 70/538 ff., each recalculated to find the prime-cost value of the assortment exchanged for slaves or wax. Ivory from the same source is for undifferentiated ivory. The median between average prices for large and small ivory this decade was £50.

18. French quantities carried from table A15.5, accepting data of either 1784 or 1786-88 as the annual average when the other shows no data, otherwise the mean of the four years. British quantities carried from appendix 11.

19. Data from appendix 11.

20. Durand, *Sénégal*, 2:45. Several lower prices are quoted at this period but they are either ambiguous or clearly the price paid in Gajaaga. Captain Heatley reported that the price on the lower Gambia was too high to make shipment to Europe profitable. (Evidence for Board of Trade Report, part 1.)

21. Annual average 1786-88, from memoranda on exports in C6 19.

22. Mean of three reports for this decade giving prices paid African merchants on lower Senegal or Gambia. See table A8.1.

23. Capt. Heatly, Board of Trade Report, part 1.

99

Table A15.7
Official Statistics of Senegambian Exports

Exports:
  a Exports to France only, in the category "commerce special" excluding re-
     exports from France.
  b Exports to France only, in the category "commerce général" including
     entrepôt goods and French reexports.
  c Exports of African products only, excluding reexports of European products
     toward the hinterland.
  d Entrepôt reporting, including at least some European goods exported to
     other parts of Africa.

Year	Senegal and dependencies (1,000 fr)	£ Equivalent	Gambia (£ sterling)	Total
1817	591	23,876	---	
1818 (1st 1/2 yr. only)	1,039	42,911	---	
1819	636a	27,094	---	
1820	612a	23,501	---	
1821	507a	19,469	---	
1822	1,072a	41,594	---	
1823	1,775c	68,160	57,651c	125,811
1824	2,371c	68,160	---	
1825	1,548b	59,134	---	
1826	1,861b	71,835	---	
1827	2,212b	86,047	---	
1828	3,448b	134,817	60,302c	195,119
1829	2,465	96,628	65,130c	161,758
1830	3,071	118,234	50,765c	168,999
1831	3,314b	129,909	38,434c	168,343
1832	2,419c	93,132	92,648c	185,780
1833	2,375c	91,913	66,221c	158,134
1834	2,763c	107,757	74,633c	182,390
1835	2,904c	112,675	91,368d	204,043
1836	4,051c	157,179	147,732d	304,911
1837	5,023c	194,892	138,226d	333,118
1838	7,468d	289,758	129,498d	419,256
1839	6,779d	265,737	162,789d	428,526
1840	4,921c	192,411	124,669d	317,080
1841	4,148c	161,772	115,824d	277,596
1842	3,551c	137,779	149,113	286,892

Year	St. Louis	Gorée	£ Equivalent	Gambia (£ sterling)	Total
1843	2,094c	1,393c	134,947	134,513d	269,460
1844	2,721c	804c	136,770	136,745d	273,515
1845	7,710c	583	320,110	154,816d	474,926
1846	5,673c	700c	245,998	163,082d	409,080
1847	5,096c	608c	221,315	178,112d	399,427
1848	2,257c	814c	118,234	158,190d	276,424
1849	2,469c	316c	110,008	107,802d	217,810
1850	2,471c	320c	109,965	142,336d	252,301

Sources: Senegal and dependencies: 1817-18, ANF-OM, Sénégal XIII 72; 1819-
23 and 1825-31, Duchon-Doris, *Toiles bleues*, p. 64; 1832 onward, *Statistiques
coloniales*, annual volumes. Gambia: 1823, CO 267/93, f. 9; 1828 onward, Gambia
Blue Books, annual series, CO 90.

Table A15.8
Senegambian Exports by Value, 1832-50

Colonial export statistics modified so as to give estimated total value of all
African products exported by sea through the European trade enclaves in Senegambia

Year	Senegal and dependencies, sterling equivalent	The Gambia, sterling	Total
1832	£ 93,132	£ 96,039	£189,171
1833	91,913	65,408	157,321
1834	107,757	71,806	179,563
1835	112,675	65,699	178,374
1836	157,179	115,722	272,901
1837	194,892	106,113	301,005
1838	289,758	101,968	391,726
1839	265,737	120,398	386,135
1840	192,411	106,628	299,039
1841	161,772	98,475	260,247
1842	137,779	106,961	244,740
1843	134,947	113,869	248,816
1844	136,770	122,349	259,119
1845	320,110	131,446	451,556
1846	245,998	149,282	395,280
1847	221,315	185,952	407,267
1848	118,234	141,497	259,731
1849	110,008	97,041	207,049
1850	109,965	151,656	261,621

Sources: *Statistiques coloniales,* annual volumes; Gambia Blue Books, annual
series, CO 90, missing data for 1848 supplied by interpolation. Gambia figures
revised as indicated on p. 91 in appendix 15 above.

Table A15.9
Principal Senegambian Exports, Annual Averages for the 1830's

Commodity	Exported by: French	English	Total exports	Unit value in sterling prime-cost	Total value	Per cent
Gold (kgs)	70.8	15.7	86.5	£118.55	£ 10,255	3.0
Gum (tons)	3,143	247	3,390	72.49	245,741	71.8
Hides (no.)	492	887	1,379	20.00	27,580	8.1
Ivory (tons)	13.8	12.7	26.5	363.50	9,633	2.8
Slaves (no.)	400	---	400	16.26	6,504	1.9
Wax (tons)	50	248	298	113.71	33,886	9.9
Peanuts (tons)	---	693 undecorticated		11.81		
		31 decorticated		19.68	8,794	2.6
Total					£342,393	100.0

Sources for quantities: Appendix 11, except for slaves. For estimate of
illicit slave trade to Saint Louis and Gorée, see chapter 5, pp. 187-96.
Sources for prices: Gold: Mean of prices cited in Oddonnateur's Report,
Galam Company, 1833-34, and *Statistiques coloniales,* 1844. Gum: Price used in
calculating Gambian export data in Gambia Blue Books, annual series, 1836-40,
preferred to equivalent in *Statistiques coloniales* (£54), which had become by
this period an "official" price repeated year after year. Hides: Gambia price
preferred to Senegalese price on the basis of weight. Ivory: Mean between
Gambian (£450.40) and Senegalese (£276.60) customs figures, averaged over 1836-40.
Slaves: Mean of quotations of Saint Louis and Gorée prices for 1836 and 1847 in
table A8.1. Wax: Mean between Gambian (£141.50) and Senegalese (£85.91) prices
used in customs reporting, 1836-40. Peanuts: Gambian prices used for customs
reporting 1836-40.

trade are somewhat easier, since the percentage distribution of imports and exports has already been established for various periods. These data give the makeup of the "basket" of goods whose changing prices over time are to be examined. The difficult problem is to supply prices for enough goods over long enough runs of time to make a significant estimate possible—and it has to be said again that the calculations rest on such a weak data base that they must be thought of as estimates rather than hard numerical facts.

Export prices and quantities have already been established at least in the form of annual averages over approximate decades at half-century intervals. Neither the source data nor the form of calculation justifies trying to push export prices to the point of creating an annual series before the nineteenth century.

Import prices have been established for a few selected commodities, but the short list of iron, silver, arms, powder, brandy, and guinées is not enough of the whole to serve as a basis for a general index of import prices. A reasonably reliable general index of import prices in annual series can be constructed for two different periods in Senegambian history before 1750. The first of these applies fully only to prices of goods sold on the Gambia, but it runs from 1671 to 1704 and again from 1727 through 1741. The list of commodities is of the fifteen most-imported commodities. The prices used were as nearly as possible f.o.b. prices at a European port—normally British, but Amsterdam for some commodities, and sometimes adjusted to account for systematic differences between prices at different ports, when changing from the data of one port to another.

Although any single-year prices mentioned in the literature were recorded, the sources actually used were three. The Royal African Company maintained a series of records called Invoice Books, Outward (T 70/910 ff.), which were continuous for the period 1673-1704 and again for 1715-30, and once again (this time for the Company of Merchants Trading to Africa) from 1750 onward. K. G. Davies used these records in his *Royal African Company* (pp. 350-57), where he reported prices and annual values for 1673-1704. As a result, an annual average price can be deduced for that period. Before 1673 and after 1727, the price recorded was the price of each commodity at the first occurrence in the calendar year (beginning January 1 even under the old-style calendar). This is not an average, but it should maintain a consistent seasonal bias.

The second source was the series of Gambia account books, not as systematic as the Invoice Books, Outward, but containing copies of London invoices of goods bound for the Gambia (in the 1680's) and having prime cost information at other periods, especially 1727-41, when the Gambia accounts were especially full. In this case too, the price recorded was the first occurrence in the calendar year.

The third source of price data was the compilation in N. W. Posthumus, *Prices in Holland*—mainly of Amsterdam prices. These are here translated into sterling at the par value of Dutch and English silver content in coinage; both currencies were then on a silver standard.

Whichever of the three sources was used for a particular period, the record was not equally complete for all commodities. Missing data were normally filled in by interpolation, but the nature of the evidence is moderately self-correcting. The important imports, like iron, were frequently reported (and an iron price is missing for only two years). The record is also accurate for brass and pewter, but a low-frequency import like "red cloth" was reported by price in only twelve years, which meant that more years were interpolated than not. The self-correcting element is the fact that weighting in the final index placed greatest emphasis on price changes of the important and well-reported commodities.

Some of the individual commodities pose special problems. Guns, for example, came in several different qualities. This causes no trouble in the period covered by Davies' survey (1671-1704), because we have the average cost per gun—not the differing costs of muskets on one hand and "fowling pieces" on the other. The flint-lock introduced later as the ordinary "trading gun" was an item reasonably standard over time and constituting the great bulk of Senegambian imports of firearms, which means that its price can be taken as representative of all firearms prices from the 1720's onward.

In the bead category, ordinary glass beads were generally sold at the same price per hundredweight, regardless of style or color, though some varieties went for higher prices. The ordinary price, however, can serve as a base price for beadware in general. Among specialized stones, coral was sold by weight and poses no serious problem, but amber occurs on the account books as "large" or "small," with a premium of about 60 per cent for large. It is therefore possible to follow the price of the "large" category as representative, but without being absolutely certain that the size of "large" was constant over time. Crystal also came in different qualities, bearing different numbers, and the RAC handled at least nine different kinds in the late seventeenth century. The relative prices of different qualities, however, remained reasonably constant, and it is possible to take no. 22 as a representative price for crystal in general. This choice follows from the fact that quality numbers dropped out after the 1720's, but a period of overlap shows no. 22 selling for the same price as the undifferentiated stones.

Cutlery was like crystal, with several different types selling at different prices, and the solution is the same—to find a single type with a fairly constant price which could be taken as representative. In the sevententh century the commonest item was simply the trade sword, but sometime between 1704 and 1727, "sword" came to refer to a more expensive item with brass mountings, and the commonest utilitarian blade was sold as a "cutlass." Even so, the price of trade swords was not reported often in the seventeenth century, and it seemed more accurate to base cutlery as a broader category on Davies' data for the average price of knives. After 1727, this base was adjusted to cutlasses by reference to the relative prices of knives and trade swords in the six seventeenth-century years in which prices were reported for both.

Textiles were the most uncertain of all. The same names are

Table A15.10

Import Price Index and Price Relatives of Major Gambian Imports, 1671-1704, 1727-41

(Average price 1683-85 = 100. Price index weighted in proportion to average import values, 1683-85.)

Year	Metals & Metalware				Textiles			Cutlery & Weapons			Beads & semiprecious stones				Spirits	Index
	Iron	Copper	Brass	Pewter	Red cloth	Tap-seals	Sile-sias	Guns	Powder	Swords	Beads	Coral	Amber	Crystal		
1671	114	103	97	105	101	101	146	81	136	83	80	141	115	126	96	106
1672	122	107	99	107	101	103	171	85	141	87	82	145	130	145	102	113
1673	118	103	92	104	101	99	134	78	128	77	75	135	107	138	93	105
1674	111	106	70	130	101	97	119	90	128	64	126	134	107	138	96	110
1675	113	117	159	122	101	95	122	96	128	64	105	131	126	126	96	110
1676	109	115	80	128	101	83	80	90	119	66	111	127	126	120	102	108
1677	109	111	89	127	101	88	73	93	117	73	113	125	134	120	102	110
1678	109	107	100	126	101	92	73	97	115	83	115	124	118	113	105	109
1679	109	102	112	125	101	97	85	101	112	92	118	125	115	120	96	109
1680	109	98	120	125	101	101	91	108	111	109	121	124	95	113	93	108
1681	99	104	100	123	101	107	117	97	106	93	125	146	92	107	99	106
1682	92	103	97	113	101	100	92	103	95	106	116	106	84	101	96	99
1683	96	102	98	106	101	121	101	96	97	106	101	97	93	102	93	98
1684	95	101	109	98	101	103	131	92	110	98	98	97	87	100	93	96
1685	108	97	93	96	101	77	69	112	93	97	100	106	121	97	113	105
1686	103	100	99	96	101	89	64	118	97	102	95	109	105	107	71	97
1687	97	100	98	97	101	101	58	126	95	99	93	97	99	105	75	94
1688	86	100	101	97	101	112	53	131	94	94	92	84	93	110	94	93
1689	99	96	104	92	101	110	61	130	122	91	92	101	92	107	121	101
1690	97	93	122	88	101	116	46	139	140	89	102	85	92	101	147	104
1691	104	111	108	117	101	115	45	173	160	92	143	95	92	101	163	116
1692	103	106	105	109	101	115	46	163	197	91	127	93	93	97	211	120

(continued)

104

Year																
1693	117	185	101	134	112	99	95	212	164	47	101	101	88	112	107	96
1694	126	176	113	172	108	114	95	129	159	44	112	101	94	95	106	112
1695	135	156	126	183	127	146	97	177	158	61	121	101	101	136	115	122
1696	134	160	145	191	104	118	100	210	139	110	117	101	88	133	124	125
1697	143	179	145	191	115	157	99	187	160	189	113	101	103	129	132	123
1698	130	169	138	191	106	134	94	92	136	52	109	101	96	128	142	105
1699	124	150	132	189	118	122	92	102	127	49	96	101	94	128	137	102
1700	122	144	132	187	118	112	91	112	121	49	90	101	92	128	133	100
1701	128	144	126	229	131	102	89	122	117	50	213	101	92	124	130	99
1702	124	128	126	229	144	108	89	177	131	48	112	101	91	118	116	91
1703	127	131	120	229	148	132	85	248	158	49	106	101	81	129	125	95
1704	128	134	120	177	135	148	83	253	148	49	92	112	109	128	123	112
1727	121	103	117	101	126	72	83	227	90	86	103	104	106	125	115	169
1728	113	92	111	101	169	72	80	208	90	83	103	98	101	111	112	160
1729	107	81	110	101	128	75	80	185	89	93	103	98	82	91	122	116
1730	100	70	110	101	231	75	80	179	89	86	103	104	79	86	133	104
1731	99	56	106	101	192	75	80	179	89	89	103	111	85	74	134	99
1732	95	52	110	101	231	52	76	114	88	93	103	111	85	82	134	108
1733	96	63	110	101	202	44	80	121	79	93	103	109	85	83	133	108
1734	96	63	110	101	213	45	80	118	89	93	103	109	85	86	128	106
1735	98	58	104	101	218	46	80	126	89	93	103	112	89	90	125	103
1736	99	60	104	101	252	55	80	125	89	93	103	112	85	92	121	100
1737	98	58	110	101	263	54	67	119	89	79	103	100	84	115	115	99
1738	99	61	110	101	256	75	76	116	77	76	103	95	83	115	109	99
1739	97	68	108	101	234	77	67	138	78	68	103	96	84	115	89	99
1740	104	97	123	101	189	75	76	215	78	69	103		85	115	93	111
1741	101	90	109	101	158	75	80	184	78		103				91	113

used again and again, but without assurance that they represent
the same commodity or the same size, since much of the textile
trade was by the piece rather than by length of bolt. For that
matter, hand-loomed cloths from India varied somewhat in quality
from piece to piece. All one can hope for on this score is that
the variation, and hence the errors, will be random.
The value of random change appears as an assist in another way.
The import index in table A15.10 was base-weighted with the years
1683-85 equal to 100. As an experiment, however, the same data
were rerun current-weighted with the import percentages of the
1730's equal to 100. The differences in the final price index
were not insignificant.

AN IMPORT INDEX COMPARING THE 1730'S WITH THE 1780'S

The data are not sufficient to continue the annual index number
for imports beyond the 1730's, but it is possible to use averages
over longer periods of time to compare the European cost of the
bundle of Senegambian imports, as it was in the 1730's, with the
cost of that same bundle as it had become by the 1780's. This
means that the new index number will not be continuous with the
series based in the 1680's, but will begin again with the 1730's
as 100.
Prices present more problems in this period than they do in the
previous interval, partly because French prices can now be taken
into account as they could not be earlier. Wherever possible,
Posthumus's data in *Prices in Holland* were preferred to either
French or English information, not merely because Holland had a
more "neutral" European price than either of the other two, but
also because both still bought a fair amount of their goods for
the Africa trade from the Dutch. In table A15.11, iron, gunpowder,
and brandy are all measured by the Amsterdam price. Silver is
allowed a slight adjustment to compensate for a small change in
the silver content of the Spanish dollar, since it circulated by
tale rather than weight. Brass, pewter, and arms were measured
by changes in the average invoice price, London, as indicated by
either the RAC Invoice Books or the Gambia accounts of the Company
of Merchants.
Bead prices are especially difficult in the 1780's because of
the great variety of types and names. A London invoice price is
used for the 1730's, and a French price for 1777 (from D. Rinchon,
Le trafic négrier, p. 103) is considered representative enough for
the 1780's. It is, in fact, quite close to the price of beads in
either the 1730's or the 1830's, so that all it does is to confirm no change.
Textiles again raise the problem of finding or constructing
an index broadly representative of a large category of goods. The
data are too incomplete to follow many individual cloths over a
significant period of time, but a generalized index for European
textile prices can be made by using those that turn up most con-
sistently and with the greatest appearance of uniformity—the
English price of silesias weighted at 50 per cent of the total,

Table A15.11
Index Numbers of Senegalese Import Prices for the 1780's
(Average price of 1730's = 100)

Iron	149
Silver	99
Brassware	114
European cloth	108
Indian cloth	198
Firearms	142
Gunpowder	137
Beads	101
Spirits	127
General index base-weighted for base 1730's	134

Sources: See pp. 163-64 of primary volume. Weights for the
1730's following table 8.3, adjusted to drop copper, which no
longer has price data in the 1780's.

Table A15.12
Index Numbers of Senegalese Import Prices for the 1830's
(Base prices of the 1780's = 100)

Iron	120
Silver	100
European textiles	29
Indian textiles	63
Firearms	123
Gunpowder	93
Beads	103
Spirits	80
Tobacco	153
General index base-weighted for base 1780's	83

Sources: For weights, table 8.3. See text pp. 161-65 of primary volume for price sources.

with the French price of woolen cloth and linen cloth respectively
making up 25 per cent each. Silesia prices (with occasional interpolation for missing data) are available from the RAC Invoice
Books, Outward, while the French prices have been assembled by
C. E. Labrousse.[3] Indian textiles can be handled in a similar
way by taking the unweighted mean of the prices of the two most
common types with prices in annual series—tapseals and niconees—
again from the RAC invoice books.[4]

AN IMPORT PRICE INDEX FOR SENEGAMBIA
COMPARING THE 1780'S WITH THE 1830'S

The lack of an adequate sample of Senegambian imports in the
1780's is a major obstacle to carrying the import price index
forward to the 1830's. The basket of imported commodities, on
the other hand, was relatively constant over the short run—even
over the long run, compared to the export basket. No great vio-
lence will therefore be done by simply assuming that the shift
from the proportions of the 1730's to those of the 1830's would
have been gradual and that the 1780's will be fairly represented
by the mean.

Prices for representative commodities can follow the method used
for measuring change over other intervals, but with a few special
problems. Brandy was no longer an adequate measure for the price
of spirits, since the English had switched over to grain spirits
or rum, which was just as acceptable in Senegambia as the more expensive brandy. The French, however, continued to sell brandy,
and its price, landed in Saint Louis in 1836-40, was almost exactl
what it had been in Amsterdam a half-century earlier, though the
price of rum or other spirits in Bathurst had dropped to index 59.
In this and other instances of price difference between Bathurst
and Saint Louis, the index for the 1830's is taken at the mean
of the Saint Louis and Bathurst prices as indicated by customs
valuations in *Statistiques coloniales* and the Gambia Blue Books
respectively for the years 1836-40. The prices of arms, gunpowder
and spirits in table A15.12 are so derived. The Amsterdam price
. of iron was retained as the best general measure, and the price of
Virginia tobacco in bond in London is accepted as a general measure of changing tobacco prices, though the tobacco actually sold
in Senegambia by American ships at the end of the period was markedly cheaper.[5] Since a French price was used as the general price
for glass beads in the 1780's, the Saint Louis price is accepted
as representative for the 1830's. For guinées as well, the Saint
Louis price is taken as the best measure, the mean of varying quotations found in the literature for the 1780's serving as a base.

A general indicator for the price of European textiles again
poses a problem. A very good series was compiled in nineteenth-
century England, giving the prices actually paid for standard grey
printing cloth by a firm of calico printers in Mayfield from 1812-
60,[6] and this is taken as the indicator for the European costs of
machine-made cottons, which became the greatest part of the European cloth imported by Senegambia. The fact that the index begins

only in 1812 is not as serious as it might have been, because
nothing very spectacular happened to the price of textiles over
the period back to the 1780's. It is therefore more legitimate
that it might be otherwise to use the price of British linen to
fill out the series from the 1780's to 1812-16, where the five-
year average prices of the two textiles can be used to link the
linen series to the cotton series that follows.

One source of inaccuracy in this calculation may lie in the
fact that the prices of spirits, beads, gunpowder, and guns as
recorded for the 1789's were the prime costs in Europe, while
those recorded for the 1830's were taken from the Senegalese
customs records. Without further specification, these might be
taken for c.i.f. prices. On the other hand, a comparison of
scattered European quotations found in the literature with these
Senegalese values shows no systematic difference between French
and Senegalese values. The subject remains confused, but appar-
rently the Senegalese customs officials were still doing as their
eighteenth-century predecessors had done and valuing goods from
Europe at their European prices. With some remaining uncertainty,
therefore, these prices are accepted as equivalent to f.o.b. at a
French port and not c.i.f. in Senegal.

THE ANNUAL SERIES OF IMPORT PRICE INDICES, EXPORT PRICE
INDICES, AND TERMS OF TRADE, 1823-50

Tables A15.13 and A15.14 present annual indices and terms of
trade calculations for the period covered by the *Statistiques
coloniales* and the Gambia Blue Books. Import price data are
those used by each colonial government in reporting its imports
for these years, with interpolations for missing years. In general, the import prices were not very different between the two
colonies even though the baskets of imports used to weight the
total import index for each territory were somewhat different.
Since data are available for only six major Gambian imports, the
eight Senegalese imports are shown on table A15.13 for representative prices of the European products used in both.

The export price indices are also independently constructed, but
with different prices for the two colonies, rather than a single
representative price as in table A15.12. Data for Saint Louis,
however, begin only in 1832, so that hides and wax prices before
1832 are taken at the Gambian levels indicated in the Blue Books.
Gum and ivory prices for Senegal 1823-31, on the other hand, are
taken from occasional scattered quotations in the literature,
plus interpolation.

The export price indices for the two colonies differ from each
other mainly because of the differing pattern of exports. Beeswax, for example, was 39 per cent of Gambian exports and only 4
per cent of Senegalese. Gum, which was 78 per cent of Senegalese
exports, was only 25 per cent of Gambian.

Table A15.13

Price Indices of Sengambian Imports, 1780's and 1823-50 Annually
(1836-40 = 100)

Year	Unweighted Senegal commodity indices								Weighted import indices by colony	
	Iron	Indian textiles	European textiles	Firearms	Gunpowder	Beads	Brandy	Tobacco	Senegal	Gambia
1780's	150	160	404	68	98	97	100	64	211	---
1823	124	173	167	107	116	81	122	83	153	105
1824	150	173	174	111	121	81	122	75	155	108
1825	218	173	150	117	123	81	122	102	150	120
1826	178	174	126	112	121	81	122	89	143	111
1827	141	138	119	108	118	81	122	75	122	104
1828	126	155	117	102	117	81	122	65	129	98
1829	112	91	105	96	113	81	122	74	95	95
1830	101	87	104	89	98	81	115	69	92	87
1831	98	95	106	85	119	81	107	65	96	91
1832	122	106	102	86	118	81	100	66	100	90
1833	125	102	106	91	116	81	98	72	100	95
1834	90	100	111	93	114	79	98	80	100	95
1835	80	96	121	95	112	79	98	90	102	97
1836	80	94	119	101	109	78	100	98	101	112
1837	113	104	93	106	106	87	100	81	98	101
1838	113	104	100	101	98	100	101	86	101	94
1839	81	105	103	95	93	112	101	136	106	104
1840	113	92	86	98	95	123	100	99	94	91
1841	61	91	86	90	97	102	100	85	90	87
1842	49	80	72	83	92	120	98	61	80	78
1843	41	75	74	81	100	117	93	60	79	80
1844	46	72	74	78	93	111	94	56	76	77
1845	74	71	71	80	93	107	121	54	74	81
1846	77	73	65	85	93	104	123	60	76	81
1847	81	67	68	86	92	105	87	60	74	83
1848	60	62	58	74	93	128	78	67	68	78
1849	51	64	64	69	93	123	78	74	70	79
1850	48	38	72	66	96	120	78	98	61	84

Table A15.14

Price Indices of Sengambian Exports, 1780's and 1823-50 Annually

(1836—40 = 100)

| Year | Unweighted commodity indices | | | | Weighted indices and terms of trade, by colony | | | |
| | | | | | Senegal | | Gambia | |
	Gum	Hides	Ivory	Beeswax	Export index	Terms of trade	Export index	Terms of trade index
1780's	47	5	9	74	41		--	--
1823	115	62	61	111	106	69	98	93
1824	119	67	80	113	110	71	103	95
1825	125	80	100	116	117	78	110	92
1826	117	77	111	106	111	77	104	94
1827	112	75	107	96	106	86	98	94
1828	103	75	113	87	99	77	92	94
1829	95	75	153	87	94	99	94	99
1830	84	100	119	111	89	96	105	121
1831	66	87	86	139	73	76	106	117
1832	65	95	66	100	71	71	89	99
1833	64	100	86	60	70	70	75	80
1834	64	100	86	60	70	70	75	79
1835	64	100	87	69	70	69	79	81
1836	124	100	88	97	118	117	107	95
1837	123	100	116	97	119	121	108	107
1838	77	101	98	97	82	81	96	102
1839	86	100	98	104	89	84	101	97
1840	89	100	100	104	92	98	102	112
1841	92	100	98	100	94	103	100	115
1842	77	100	98	73	81	100	85	109
1843	77	98	98	100	82	104	96	119
1844	115	99	98	104	112	148	108	140
1845	122	97	98	104	117	157	109	135
1846	62	100	98	97	70	93	91	113
1847	67	100	98	97	74	100	93	112
1848	67	105	98	98	75	110	94	122
1849	66	100	98	97	74	105	92	118
1850	64	100	98	97	72	117	92	110

NOTES

1. From "Notes prises avec M. de la Bruë," 18 July 1751, ANF, C6 13.

2. Such as C. F. Gaignet de Laulnais, *Guide de commerce* (Paris, 1764), p. 312, and L'Abbé Demanet, *Nouvelle histoire de l'Afrique française,* 2 vols. (Paris, 1767), 1:251-54.

3. C. E. Labrousse, *Esquisse du mouvement des prix et des revenue en France au xviiie siècle,* 2 vols. (Paris, 1933), 2:231-32, 331-32.

4. Bafts or pièces de Guinée would have been the logical touchstone for Indian textile prices, but I was unable to find any reliable price for any period in or near the 1730's. The rise of 220 per cent from 1718 to the 1780's, however (table A15.3), is not far from the rise of 198 per cent in the Tapseal-Niconee index between the 1730's and the 1780's.

5. T. Tooke, *A History of Prices and of the State of Circulation from 1792 to 1856,* 6 vols. (1838-57; New York, 1928), 2:418, 3:298. See also G. E. Brooks, Jr., *Yankee Traders, Old Coasters, and African Middlemen* (Boston, 1970), p. 147.

6. Alderman Neild, "An Account of the Price of Printing Cloth and Upland Cotton from 1812 to 1860 A.D.," *Journal of the Royal Statistical Society,* 24:491-97 (1861).

BIBLIOGRAPHY
&
INDEX

BIBLIOGRAPHY

A NOTE ON THE SOURCES

This study has drawn on the three different kinds of historical evidence—reports of European travelers or visitors, the archives of colonial governments or European trading companies, oral traditions and Arabic documents originating with Senegambians. Of these, the travelers' reports present no bibliographic problem. Most take the form of printed books and are listed below.

The others are in manuscript form in the European archives and libraries or in the hands and heads of private individuals in Senegal and the Gambia. Some of these do present bibliographic problems. One kind of European account that was especially common with the French of the eighteenth century was the long official report on twenty to one hundred sheets of paper or more, with some of the qualities of a book or pamphlet but destined for official use only. These were often copied over and over again, so that several are now found in different archives in Paris, filed in several different ways, and in the Bibliothèque nationale as well. They are not listed separately in the bibliography below because they are reasonably well catalogued by Patricia Carson in *Materials for West African History in French Archives* (London, 1968). Several have been abstracted and published in the collection of J. Machat, *Documents sur les établissements français et l'Afrique occidentale au xviiie siècle,* or as annexes to secondary studies like those of Boubacar Barry or André Delcourt. Others have been printed as journal contributions and are thus listed in the bibliography below, and still others are in the process of annotation for publication in the near future.[*]

A second kind of long manuscript is also found in the French archives. This is the secondary account, historical or descriptive,

---

[*]Such as the "Journal d'un voyiage fait en Bambouc en 1744" by Pierre Félix David, being edited by André Delcourt from a manuscript in the Municipal Library of Rouen, and "Relation de Bambouc" by Claude Boucard (1729), being edited by P. D. Curtin and Jean Boulègue from a document in the Archive de la Marine, Paris.

115

often of book length. These are not so often found in multiple
copies, and they are listed in the bibliography below along with
more recent secondary works still in manuscript, typescript, or
mimeographed form.

Both Senegal and the Gambia have well-run and well-organized
archival services, with a variety of finding aids, including
published indices in the case of Senegal. But they are both
limited to the nineteenth century, because of the inter-European
warfare at the end of the eighteenth which destroyed virtually
all the documentation not carried off by the one or the other of
the two contending parties. This means that documentation for
the eighteenth century and earlier and originating with Europeans
is mainly to be found in Europe—in France in the central Archives
nationales in rue des Francs-Bourgeois for the eighteenth century,
or the Overseas Section in rue Oudinot for the post-Napoleonic
period. In London the equivalent depository is the Public Record
Office, where the records of the trading companies are found in
the Treasury series and those of the Gambian governments are in
the Colonial Office series. A few documents, it goes without
saying, are found scattered here and there outside these main
depositories. The Archives de la Marine in Paris, for example,
holds some important reports of the eighteenth century, though
its official responsibilities begin with 1870. In England, some
of the minutes of the Royal African Company's Gambian Council for
parts of 1723 and 1729 are found among the Rawlinson Papers, c.
745-47 of the Bodleian Library, Oxford, a collection otherwise
concerned with the Gold Coast between 1681 and 1699.

The very fact that some documents are known to be outside the
main archival centers of England and France suggests that even
more could be found by diligent search—not merely there, but in
Portugal and the Netherlands as well. Study of some historical
problems, such as of Europeans overseas at a particular time and
place, would require an exhaustive search for documentary evidence. The search for evidence about the Senegambian economy
over a long period and in the records of another society imposed
other conditions. This was an "archive-extensive" task, with many
hours of reading about European activities for each bit of hard
information about the African economy that lay beyond the European
enclaves. In this situation, the richest of the French and English
colonial archives had to be treated as though they were large
samples. Beyond these large collections other data surely exist,
but the yield in evidence per hour of search was no longer enough
to justify the expenditure in time.

Evidence generated by the Senegambians in Arabic documents or
in oral traditions was much richer than the European record in
its treatment of Senegambian society, but it was relatively si-
lent about economic aspects of that society. Paper disintegrates
in a tropical climate, so that written documents survive only if
someone takes the trouble to recopy at least once a century.
Arabic works on law or religion were worth copying. Old account
books were not. Some documents that bear on the political or
social history of trade networks have nevertheless survived and
could be borrowed from their owners for photocopying. My

collection of Jahaanke documents of this kind is held by the
Institut fondamental de l'Afrique noire in Dakar as the "Fonds
Curtin," and microfilms of the collection are available for loan
or duplication at the Center for Research Libraries, 5721 South
Cottage Grove Avenue, Chicago, Illinois 60637.

The quantity of surviving oral data bearing on distant economic
history is also much less than that of European records, but it
was valuable for this study in hundreds of ways that cannot be
reflected in footnote references. Direct evidence about economic
institutions extends no further back than the late nineteenth
century, but historical narrations about more distant periods
carry an even more valuable, if indirect, understanding of probable social systems and social values of the more distant past.
To write the economic history of Senegambia in the eighteenth
century without listening to the minstrels tell the life of
Samba Gelaajo Jegi would be like writing the economic history of
nineteenth-century England without reading Dickens's novels.

My field collection is on deposit as the Curtin Collection of
the oral traditions of Bundu at IFAN in Dakar and at the African
Studies Association, Center for African Oral Data, Archive of
Traditional Music, Maxwell Hall, Indiana University, Bloomington.
The ASA center can make an index available, and individual tapes
can circulate and be duplicated at cost. The originals are in
Pulaar, Soninke, Malinke, Jahaanke, and Arabic. Most of those
relevant to this study are accompanied by an oral translation
into French, also on tape.

UNPUBLISHED THESES AND OTHER
MANUSCRIPT SECONDARY AUTHORITIES

Adanson, Michel. "Pièces instructives concernant l'île de Goré
    voisine du Cap-verd en Afrike, avec un Projet et des vues
    utiles relativement au nouvel établissement de Kaiène." Dated
    May-June 1, 1963. ANF, C6 14.
Anonymous. "Renseignemens sur le Sénégal et autres etablissemens
    français à la côte d'Afrique d'après les manuscrits déposes dans
    le bureau de l'Administration Coloniale (depuis la conquête
    du Sénégal en 1779 à ce jour, 1801)." Dated Germinal An IX,
    ANF, C6 27.
Austen, Ralph. "The Composition of Dutch-Cameroon Trade in the
    Mid-18th Century: Its Social and Political Effects." Paper
    presented at the University of Chicago Workshop in Economic
    History, October 26, 1973, intended for ultimate publication
    in the *Annales de la faculté des lettres et sciences humaines*
    of the Université de Yaoundé, Cameroun.
Barry, Boubacar. "Le Royaume du Walo, 1659-1859." Ph.D. dis-
    sertation, 3rd cycle, University of Paris, 1970. Subsequently
    published; see "Published Works."
Berkis, Alexander V. "The Reign of Duke James of Courland (1623-
    1682)." Ph.D. dissertation, University of Wisconsin, 1956.
    Subsequently published; see "Published Works."
Boulègue, Jean. "La Sénégambie du milieu du xve siècle au début

du xviie siècle." Ph.D. dissertation, 3rd cycle, University of Paris, 1969. Published version in press.

Brown, William Allen. "The Caliphate of Hamdullahi, ca. 1818-1864: A Study in African History and Tradition." Ph.D. dissertation, University of Wisconsin, 1969.

Cissoko, Sékéné Mody. "Introduction à l'histoire des Mandigues de l'ouest: L'empire de Kabou (xvie-xixe siècle)." Paper presented at the Conference on Manding Studies, School of Oriental and African Studies, University of London, 1972.

Coifman, Victoria Bomba. "History of the Wolof State of Jolof until 1860 Including Comparative Data from the Wolof State of Walo." Ph.D. dissertation, University of Wisconsin, 1969.

Colvin, Lucie Anne Gallistel. "Kajor and its Diplomatic Relations with Saint-Louis du Sénégal, 1763-1861." Ph.D. dissertation, Columbia University, 1971.

Diallo, Thierno. "Sur l'origine et la disposition du peuple peul avant le xixe siècle." Ph.D. dissertation, 3rd cycle, University of Paris, 1964.

Dieng, Doudou. "Cercle de Bakel." CRDS, Saint Louis du Sénégal.

Diop, Abdoulaye Sokhna. "La genèse de la royauté Gueleware au Siin et au Saalum." Paper presented at the Conference on Manding Studies, School of Oriental and African Studies, University of London, 1972.

Durand, [J. B. L.]. "Voyage du Sénégal à Galam par terre." Account of a trip made by Sieur Rubault, dated 13 June 1796, ANF, C6 19.

Duranger. "Journal du sieur Duranger, Employé de la Compagnie des Indes, au Sénégal, du 9 May, au 19. Octobre 1758." ANF, C6 14.

Guirassy, Mamba. "Etude sommaire sur la race Diakha." In the possession of the author, Ministère de l'education nationale, Dakar.

Harris, Joseph Earl. "The Kingdom of Fouta Diallon." Ph.D. dissertation, Northwestern University, 1965.

Howard, Allen M. "Big Men, Traders, and Chiefs: Power, Commerce and Spacial Change in the Sierra Leone-Guinea Plain." Ph.D. dissertation, University of Wisconsin, 1972.

Hull, Thomas, "Voyage to Bundo." 1735. Manuscript from the library of the Duke of Buccleuch.

Johnson, James P. "The Almamate of Futo Toro, 1779-1836: A Political History." Ph.D. dissertation, University of Wisconsin 1974.

Lauer, Joseph Jerome. "Rice in the History of the Lower Gambia-Geba Area." Master's thesis, University of Wisconsin, 1969.

LeBrasseur. "Détails historiques et politiques sur la religion, les moeurs, et le commerce des peuples qui habitent la côte occidentale d'Afrique." Dated June 1778. Anciens FF, BN, no. 12080.

Le Veen, E. Phillip. "British Slave Trade Suppression Policies 1821-1865: Impact and Implications." Ph.D. dissertation, University of Chicago, 1971.

M'Bow, Amadou Maktar. "Enquête préliminaire sur le village de Sénoudébou, Canton du Boundou septentrional, subdivision de

Goudiry, Cercle de Tambacounda." Mimeographed study dated May 1954 in series Térritoire du Sénégal, education de base, ANS.
Mahoney, Florence K. Omolara. "Government and Opinion in the Gambia, 1816-1901. Ph.D. dissertation, University of London, 1963. Revised version in press.
Picard, C. M. C. "Des possessions françaises en Afrique." Dated Paris, 1814. ANF, C6 28.
Quinn, Charlotte Alison. "Traditionalism, Islam, and European Expansion: The Gambia 1850-90." Ph.D. dissertation, University of California, Los Angeles, 1967. Subsequently published; see "Published Works."
Robinson, David Wallace, Jr. "Abdul Bokar Kan and the History of Futa Toro, 1853 to 1891." Ph.D. dissertation, Columbia University, 1971.
Sidibe, B. K. "The Story of Kaabu: Its Extent." Paper presented at the Conference on Manding Studies, School of Oriental and African Studies, University of London, 1972.
_____. "The Story of Kaabu: The Fall of Kaabu." Paper presented at the Conference on Manding Studies, School of Oriental and African Studies, University of London, 1972.
_____. "The Story of Kaabu: Kaabu's Relationship with the Gambian States." Paper presented at the Conference on Manding Studies, School of Oriental and African Studies, University of London, 1972.
Steff, Capitaine. "Histoire du Fouta Toro." 1913. Fonds Gaden, cahier no. 1, IFAN, Dakar.
Wane, Amadou Tamibou. "Etude sur la race toucouleur." CRDS, Saint Louis du Sénégal, document 176.
Wiedner, Donald Lawrence. "Coins and Accounts in West European and Colonial History, 1250-1936." Ph.D. dissertation, Harvard University, 1958.

PUBLISHED WORKS

Abun-Nasr, J. M. *The Tijaniyya: A Sufi Order in the Modern World.* London, 1965.
Adam, M. G. *Légendes historiques du pays de Nioro.* Paris, 1904.
Adams, J. G., F. Brigaud, Cl. Charreau, and R. Fauck. *Connaissance du Sénégal.* Fascicle 3, *Climat-Sols-Végétation.* Saint Louis du Sénégal, 1965.
Adanson, Michel. Voyage to Senegal, London, 1759. English translation of *Histoire naturelle du Sénégal.* Paris, 1751.
African Association, *Proceedings.* See Association for Promoting the Discovery of the Interior Parts of Africa, *Proceedings.*
Ahmed Ennasiri Esslaoui [Es Slawi]. *Kitab Elistiqsa [Kitab al-Istiqsa].* Translated by Eugène Fumey. In *Archives marocaines,* vols. 9 and 10. Paris, 1906.
Al-Bakri. "El-Bakrî (Cordoue 1068), Routier de l'Afrique blanche et noire du Nord-Ouest." Translated by Vincent Monteil. *BIFAN,* 30:39-116 (1968).
Alexis de Saint-Lo. *Relation du voyage au Cap Verd.* Paris and Rouen, 1637.

Allen, Roy G. D., and J. Edward Ely. *International Trade Statistics*. New York, 1953.

Alquier, P. "Saint-Louis du Sénégal sous la Révolution et l'Empire. *CEHSAOF*, 5:277-320, 411-63 (1922).

Al-Shinquiti, Ahmad Ibn Al-Amin. *El-Wasit*. Translated from Arabic by Mourad Teffahi. Saint Louis, 1953.

Alvares d'Almada, André. *Tratado breve dos rios de Guine de Cabo Verde*. First published 1594. Reedited by Luis Silveira. Lisbon, 1946.

Alvares de Andrade, Bernardino Antonio. *Planta de praça de Bissau e suas adjacentes*. Lisbon, 1952.

Ames, David. "The Rural Wolof of the Gambia." In Bohannan and Dalton, *Markets in Africa*. Pp. 29-60.

Amilhat, Pierre. "Petite chronique des Id ou Aich, héritiers guerriers des Almoravides sahariens, *Revue des études islamiques*, 10:41-130 (1937).

Anonymous. "Afrique: Notice sur le Senegal, la colonie francaise, ses dependances, les pays et les peuples environnans." *Journal des Voyages*, 37:5-27 (1828).

_____. "Un plan de colonisation du Sénégal en 1802." *Annuaire et mémoires du comite d'études historiques et scientifiques de l'AOF*, 1:130-214 (1916).

_____. *Le Sénégal et les guinées de Pondichery: Note présenté à la commission supérieure des colonies par les négotiants sénégalais*. Bordeaux, 1879.

Appia, Béatrice. "Les forgerons du Fouta Djallon." *Journal de la Société des Africanistes*, 35:317-52 (1965).

Archinard, Louis. "Fabrication de la poudre à tire par les Malinké du pays de Kita et du Fouladougou." *Revue ethnographique* 1:526-27 (1882).

Arcin, J. *Histoire de la Guinée française, Rivières du Sud, Fouta Djallon, région sud du Soudan*. Paris, 1911.

Armstrong, Robert G. *The Study of West African Languages*. Ibadan, 1964.

Arnaud, Robert. "Vestiges de la vénération du feu au Soudan." *Revue d'ethnographie et des traditions populaires*, 4:193-200 (1923).

Association for Promoting the Discovery of the Interior Parts of Africa. *Proceedings*. 2nd ed. in 2 vols. London, 1810.

Astley, Thomas. *A New General Collection of Voyages and Travels*. 4 vols. London, 1745.

Aubert, A. "Légendes historiques et traditions orales recueillies en Haute-Gambie." *CEHSAOF*, 6:384-428 (1923).

Audibert. "Rapport adressé à la commission de l'Exposition universelle réunie à Saint-Louis (Sénégal)." *Revue coloniale*, 14 (2nd series):177-211 (1855).

Ba, Amadou Hampaté. "Des Foulbé du Mali et leur culture." *Abbia*, nos. 14-15, pp. 23-54 (1966).

_____, and Lylian Kesteloot. "Da Monzon et Karta Thiéma." *Abbia* nos. 14-15:179-205 (1966).

Baillaud, Emile. *Sur les routes du Soudan*. Toulouse, 1902.

Barbot, John. *A Description of the Coasts of North and South Guinea*. N.p., 1732.

Barquissau, Raphaël. "Le Sénégal en 1788." *Academie des sciences d'outre-mer, Comptes-rendus mensuels des séances,* 20:265-72 (1960).

Barreira, Baltasar. "La description de la côte de Guinée du père Baltasar Barreira." Edited by Guy Thilmans and Nize Isabel de Moraes. *BIFAN,* 34:1-50 (1972).

Barreto, João. *Historia da Guiné.* Lisbon, 1938.

Barry, Boubacar. *Le royaume du Waalo, 1659-1859: Le Sénégal avant la conquête.* Paris, 1972.

Basset, René. *Mission au Sénégal.* Paris, 1909.

Bastard, Georges. "La voie fluviale du Sénégal." *Bulletin de la Société des études coloniale et maritime,* 23:320-23 (1899).

Bathily, Abdoulaye. "La conquête française du Haut-Fleuve (Sénégal), 1818-1887." *BIFAN,* 34:67-112 (1972).

Bathily, Ibrahima Diaman. "Notices socio-historiques sur l'ancien royaume soninké du Gadiaga." *BIFAN,* 31:31-105 (1969). Introduced and annotated by Abdoulaye Bathily.

_____. "Les Diawandos ou Diagorames: Traditions orales recueillies à Djenné, Corientzé, Ségou et Nioro." *L'Education africaine,* no. 94, pp. 173-93 (1936).

Bayol, Jean. "Voyage en Sénégambie, Haut-Niger, Bambouck, Fouta-Djallon et Grand Bélédougou, 1880-1885." *Revue maritime et coloniale,* 94:441-73; 95:72-104, 256-81, 438-66; 96:155-81, 492-559 (1887-88).

_____. "La France au Fouta-Djalon." *Revue des deux-mondes,* 54:902-32 (1882).

Béart, Charles. "Sur les Bassaris du cercle de Haute-Gambie (Sénégal)." *Notes africaines,* no. 34:24-26; no. 35:1-7 (1947).

Beaufort, E. P. "Expédition dans l'interieur de l'Afrique par la voie du Sénégal." *Journal des voyages,* 24:249-54 (1834).

Beaulieu, Augustin de. "Mémoire du voyage aux Indes orientales du Général Beaulieu." In Malchisédech Thévenot, *Collection des voyages.* 4 vols. Paris, 1664. Vol. 2.

Beaumier, Auguste. "Le choléra au Maroc, sa marche au Sahara jusqu'au Sénégal en 1868." *Bulletin de la Société de géographie de Paris,* 3 (6th ser.):281-305 (1872).

Belan, A. "L'or dans le cercle de Kédougou." *Notes africaines,* no. 31, pp. 9-12 (1946).

Belcher, Capt. "Extracts from Observations on Various Points of the West Coast of Africa, Surveyed by His Majesty's Ship *Aetna* in 1830-32." *JRGS,* 2:278-304 (1832).

Bellamy, C. V. "A West African Smelting House." *Journal of the Iron and Steel Institute,* no. 11, pp. 99-126 (1904). With analytical appendix by F. W. Harbord.

Bellamy, Dr. "Notes ethnographiques recueillies dans le Haut Sénégal." *Revue d'ethnographie,* 5:81-84 (1866).

Bellouard, P. "La gomme arabique en A.O.F." *Bois et forêts des tropiques,* 1, no. 9, pp. 3-18 (1947).

Belshaw, Cyril S. *Traditional Exchange and Modern Markets.* Englewood Cliffs, New Jersey, 1965.

Béraud-Villars, Jean. *L'empire de Gao.* Paris, 1942.

Bérenger-Féraud, L. J. B. *Recueil des contes populaires de la Sénégambie.* Paris, 1885.

_____. "Etude sur les Soninkés." *Revue d'anthropologie,* 1 (2nd series):584-606 (1878).

_____. *Les peuplades de la Sénégambie: Histoire, ethnographie, moeurs, et coutumes, legendes, etc.* Paris, 1879.

Berg, Elliot. "Backward-Sloping Labor Supply Functions in Dual Economies: The Africa Case." *Quarterly Journal of Economics,* 75:468-92 (1961).

Berkis, Alexander V. *The History of the Duchy of Courland (1561-1795).* Towson, Md., 1969.

Bertrand-Bocandé. "Notes sur la Guinée portugaise ou Sénégambie meridionale." *Bulletin de la Société de géographie de Paris,* 11 (3rd series):265-350 and 12:57-93 (1849).

Beveridge, William Henry. *Prices and Wages in England from the Twelfth to the Nineteenth Century.* London, 1939.

Blanche, Jules. "Le trafic au Sénégal à la fin du xviiie siècle." *Revue de géographie alpine,* 55:469-90 (1967).

Blaug, Marc. "The Productivity of Capital in the Lancashire Cotton Industry during the Nineteenth Century." *Economic History Review,* 13:376-78 (1961).

Boahen, A. Adu. *Britain, the Sahara, and the Western Sudan 1788-1861.* Oxford, 1964.

Boëthius, B. "Swedish Iron and Steel 1600-1955." *Scandinavian Economic History Review,* 6:144-75 (1958).

Bohannan, Paul J. "The Impact of Money on an African Subsistence Economy." *Journal of Economic History,* 19:491-503 (1959).

_____. "Some Principles of Exchange and Investment among the Tiv." *American Anthropologist,* 57:60-70 (1955).

_____ and Laura. *Tiv Economy,* London, 1968.

_____, and George Dalton, editors. *Markets in Africa.* Evanston, Ill., 1962.

Boilat, P. D. *Esquisses sénégalaises.* Paris, 1853.

Bonnel de Mezières, A. "Les Diakanké de Banisraila et du Boundou méridional (Sénégal), annoté par R. Mauny." *Notes africaines,* 16:20-24 (1949).

Boston University African Studies Program. *List of French Doctoral Dissertations on Africa, 1884-1961.* Boston, 1966.

Bouchez, Capt. "Region de Labbé." *Revue coloniale,* 2 (new series): 373-86 (1903).

Bouët-Willaumez, E. *Commerce et traites des noirs aux côtes occidentales d'Afrique.* Paris, 1848.

Boulègue, Jean. "Relation du port du fleuve Sénégal de João Barbosa, faite par João Baptista Vavanha (vers 1600)." *BIFAN,* 29:498-511 (1967).

_____. *Les luso-africains de Sénégambie.* Mimeographed. Dakar, 1972. Travaux et documents, Faculté des lettres et sciences humaines, Department d'histoire, Université de Dakar.

_____, and Benjamin Pinto-Bull. "Les relations du Cayor avec le Portugal dans la première moitié du XVIe siècle, d'après deux documents nouveaux." *BIFAN,* 28:663-67 (1966).

Boutillier, J. L., P. Cantrelle, J. Causse, C. Laurent, Th. N'Doye. *La moyenne vallée du Sénégal (étude socio-économique).* Paris, 1962.

Boyer, G. "Un peuple de l'ouest soudanais: Les Diawara."

Mémoires de l'Institut français d'Afrique noire, no. 29 (Dakar, 1953), pp. 15-123.

Braudel, F. P., and F. Spooner. "Prices in Europe from 1450 to 1750." In E. E. Rich and C. H. Wilson, *The Cambridge Economic History of Europe.* 6 vols. Cambridge, 1967. Vol. 4, pp. 374-86, 414-15.

Brasseur, Paule. *Bibliographie générale du Mali.* Dakar, 1964.

Brigaud, Félix. *Connaissance du Sénégal.* Part 2, *Hydrographie.* Saint Louis, 1961.

_____. *Histoire traditionelle du Sénégal.* Saint Louis du Sénégal, 1962.

Broeck, Pieter van den, "Voiages de Pierre van den Broeck au Cap vert, à Angola, et aux Indes orientales." In R. A. C. Renville, editor, *Recueil des voiages qui ont servi à l'établissement et aux progrès de la Compagnie des Indes Orientales.* 5 vols. Amsterdam, 1703-10. Vol. 4, pp. 306-473.

Brossard de Corbigny, P. "Exploration hydrographique de la Falémé." *Revue coloniale,* 3 (2nd series):142-51 (1858).

Brunner, Dr. Samuel. *Reise nach Senegambien und den Inseln der Grünen vorgebirges in Jahre 1838.* Berne, 1840.

Butel. "Notes sur les peuplades qui occupant les bords du Sénégal." *Revue coloniale,* 14 (2nd series):752-59 (1855).

Ca da Mosto, Alvise da. *The Voyages of Cadamosto and Other Documents on Western Africa in the Second Half of the Fifteenth Century.* Edited by G. R. Crone. London, 1937.

Caille. "Notes sur les peuples de la Mauritanie et de la Nigritie, riverains du Sénégal." *Revue coloniale,* 10:1-10 (1846).

Caillé, René. *Journal d'un voyage à Tombouctou et à Jenné dans l'Afrique centrale.* 5 vols. Paris, 1830.

Cantarelle, Pierre. "L'endogamie des populations du Fouta sénégalais." *Population,* 4:665-76 (1960).

Caroço, Jorge Vellez. *Monjur, O Gabu e a sua Historia.* Bissau, 1948.

Carreira, António. "Aspectos da influencia da cultura portuguesa na área compreendida entre o rio Senegal e o norte da Serra Leoa." *Boletim cultural da Guiné Portuguesa,* 20:373-416 (1964).

_____. *Panaria cabo-verdiano-guineense: Aspectos históricos e sócio-económicos.* Lisbon, 1968.

Carrère, Frédéric, and Paul Holle. *De la Sénégambie française.* Paris, 1855.

Carson, Patricia. *Materials for West African History in French Archives.* London, 1968.

Chambon. *Le commerce de l'Amérique par Marseille, ou explication des lettres-patentes du roi.* 2 vols. Avignon, 1764.

Chambonneau. "Relation du Sr. Chambonneau." *Bulletin de géographie historique et descriptive,* 2:308-21 (1898).

_____. "Deux textes sur le Senegal (1673-1677)." Edited by Carson I. A. Ritchie. *BIFAN,* 30:289-353 (1968).

_____. "Impressions of Senegal in the Seventeenth Century: Excerpts from Louis Chambonneau's *Treatise.*" Edited by C. I. A. Ritchie. *African Studies* (Johannesberg), 26 (no. 2, 1967):59-93.

Chataigner, Abel. "Les populations du cercle de Kêdougou." *Bulletin de la Société d'anthropologie de Paris,* 5 (11th series): 87-111 (supplementary volume for 1963).

Chevalier, Auguste. "Nos connaissances actuelles sur la géographie botanique et la flore économique du Sénégal et du Soudan." In Lasnet and others, *Une mission au Senegal*. Paris, 1900. Pp. 197-273.

_____, and E. Perrot. *Les kolatiers et les noix de kola*. Paris, 1911.

Cipolla, Carlo M. *Guns and Sails in the Early Phase of European Expansion 1400-1700*. London, 1965.

Cissoko, Sékéné Mody. "Civilisation Wolofo-Sérère au xve siècle d'après les sources portugaises." *Présence africaine*, 69:94-120 (1967).

_____. "Traits fondamentaux des sociétés du soudan occidental du xviie au début de xixe siècle." *BIFAN*, series B, 31:1-30 (1969)

_____. "La royauté (mansaya) chez les Mandigues occidentaux d'apres leurs traditions orales." *BIFAN*, 31:325-39 (1969).

_____. "Famines et épidémiques à Tombouctou et dans la boucle du Niger du xvie au xviiie siècle." *BIFAN*, 30:806-21 (1968).

Cligny, A. "Faune du Sénégal et de la Casamance." In Lasnet and others, *Une mission au Sénégal*. Paris, 1900. Pp. 277-321.

Cline, Walter. *Mining and Metallurgy in Negro Africa*. Menasha, Wis., 1937.

Coelho, Francisco de Lemos. *Duas descriçoes seisentistas da Guiné de Francisco de Lemos Coelho*. Edited by Damiao Peres. Lisbon, 1953.

Cohen, Abner. "Cultural Strategies in the Organization of Trading Diasporas." In Claude Meillassoux, ed., *The Development of Indigenous Trade and Markets in West Africa*. London, 1971. Pp. 266-84.

_____. "Politics of the Kola Trade." *Africa*, 36:18-36 (1966).

Cohen, Ronald. "Some Aspects of Institutionalized Exchange: A Kanuri Example." *CEA*, 5:353-69 (1965).

Colin, G. "Le Bambouk (Soudan occidental)." *Bulletin de la Société languedocienne de géographie*, 8:640-45 (1885).

_____. "La population de Bambouk." *Revue d'anthropologie*, 1:(3rd series):432-47 (1886).

_____. "Le Soudan occidental." *Revue maritime et coloniale*, 78:5-32 (1883).

_____. "Mes voyages au Sénégal." *Bulletin de la Société de géographie de Lille*, 1886, pp. 259-70.

Colombani, F. M. "Le Guidimaka, étude géographique, historique et religieuse." *CEHSAOF*, 14:365-432 (1931).

Cook, Scott. "The Obsolete 'Anti-Market' Mentality: A Critique of the Substantive Approach to Economic Anthropology." *American Anthropologist*, 68:323-45 (1966).

[Coste d'Arnobat, Charles-Pierre]. *Voyage au pays de Bambouc, suivi d'observations intéressantes sur les castes indiennes, sur la Hollande, et sur l'Angleteere*. Brussels, 1789.

Cultru, Pierre. *Les origines de l'Afrique occidentale: Histoire du Sénégal du xve siècle à 1870*. Paris, 1910.

Curtin, Philip D. *Africa Remembered*. Madison, 1967.

_____. *The Atlantic Slave Trade*. Madison, 1969.

_____. "Epidemiology and the Slave Trade." *Political Science Quarterly*, 83:190-216 (1968).

_____. *The Image of Africa.* Madison, 1964.

_____. "Jihad in West Africa: Early Phases and Inter-Relations in Mauritania and Senegal." *JAH,* 12:11-24 (1971).

_____. "Measuring the Atlantic Slave Trade." In Engerman and Genovese, *Race and Slavery in the Western Hemisphere.* Princeton, 1740.

_____. "Pre-Colonial Trading Networks and Traders: The Diakhanké." In Claude Meillassoux, ed., *The Development of Indigenous Trade and Markets in West Africa.* London, 1971. Pp. 228-39.

_____. "The White Man's Grave: Image and Reality, 1780-1850." *Journal of British Studies,* 1:94-110 (1961).

_____, and Jan Vansina. "Sources of the Nineteenth Century Atlantic Slave Trade." *JAH,* 5:185-208 (1964).

Daget, J., and A. Pitot. *Les barques du Moyen-Niger.* Paris, 1948.

Daget, Serge. "L'abolition de la traite des noirs en France de 1814 à 1831." *CEA,* 11:14-58 (1971).

Dalton, George. "Primitive, Archaic, and Modern Economies: Karl Polanyi's Contribution to Economic Anthropology and Comparative Economy." In June Helm, Paul Bohannan, and Marshall D. Sahlins, eds., *Essays in Economic Anthropology.* Seattle, 1965. Pp. 1-24.

_____. "Primitive Money." *American Anthropologist,* 67:44-65 (1965).

Dalziel, John M. *The Useful Plants of West Tropical Africa.* London, 1948.

Daniel, Fernand. "Etude sur les Soninké ou Sarakolé." *Anthropos,* 4:27-49 (1910).

Dapper, Olfert. *Description de l'Afrique.* Amsterdam, 1686.

_____ in G. Thilmans, ed., "Le Sénégal dans l'oeuvre de Olfried Dapper." *BIFAN,* 32:508-63 (1970).

Dardel, Pierre. *Navires et marchandises dans les ports de Rouen et du Havre au xviiie siècle.* Paris, 1963.

Dauphin, Joanne Coyle. "French Provincial Centers of Documentation and Research on Africa." *African Studies Bulletin,* 9:48-65 (1966).

Daveau, Suzanne. "La découverte du climat d'Afrique tropicale au cours des navigations portugaises (xve et début du xvie siècle)." *BIFAN,* 31:953-88 (1969).

Davenport, W. "When a Primitive and Civilized Money Meet." *Proceedings of the American Ethnological Society,* Spring Meeting Symposium 1961, pp. 64-68.

D'Avezac, [M. A. P.]. "Etudes de géographie critique sur l'Afrique intérieure occidentale." *Bulletin de la Société de géographie de Paris,* 11 (3rd series):137-252 (1849).

Davies, K. G. "The Living and the Dead: White Mortality in West Africa 1684-1732." In Engerman and Genovese, *Race and Slavery in the Western Hemisphere.* Princeton, 1740.

_____. *The Royal African Company.* London, 1957.

D'Avity, Pierre. *Déscription générale de l'Afrique . . .* Paris, 1640.

DeCrozals, Joseph. *Les Peuls: Etude d'ethnologie africaine.* Paris, 1883.

Delafosse, Maurice. "Les confrèries musulmanes et le maraboutisme dans les pays du Sénégal et du Niger." *Bulletin du Comité de l'Afrique française et renseignements coloniaux,* 1911, pp. 81-90.

_____. "Le clergé musulman de l'Afrique occidentale." *RMM,* 9:177-206.

_____. "Les débuts des troupes noires au Maroc." *Hésperis*, 3: 1-12 (1923).

_____. "L'état actual de l'Islam dans l'Afrique occidentale française." *RMM*, 11:32-53 (1910).

_____. *Haut-Sénégal-Niger*. 3 vols. Paris, 1912.

_____. "Relations du Maroc et du Soudan à travers les ages." *Hésperis*, 4:153-74 (1924).

_____. "Traditions historiques et légendaires du Soudan occidental, traduites d'un manuscrit arabe inédit." *Renseignements coloniaux et documents publiés par le comité de l'Afrique et le comité du Maroc*, 8:293-306, 325-29, 355-68 (1913). Supplement to *Afrique française* of August 1913.

_____, and H. Gaden, eds. "Chroniques du Foûta Sénégalais." *Revue du Monde Musulman*, 24, 1-114, and 25, 165-235 (1913).

D'Elbée, Sieur. "Journal du voyage du sieur d'Elbée aux isles, dans la coste de Guinée." In J. de Clodoré, *Relation de ce qui c'est passé dans les isles and terre ferme d'Amerique* . . . Paris, Gervais Clovzier, 1671. Pp. 345-494.

Delcourt, A. *La France et les établissements français au Sénégal entre 1712 et 1763*. Dakar, 1952.

Delhaye, F. "Les gîtes surifères du Bambouk (Soudan français)." *Annales de la Société géologique de Belgique*, 49:B248-B251 (1927)

Demanet, L'Abbé. *Nouvelle histoire de l'Afrique française*, 2 vols. Paris, 1767.

Deroure, Françoise. "La vie quotidienne à Saint-Louis par ses archives (1779-1809)." *BIFAN*, 26:397-439 (1964).

Désiré-Vuillemin, G. M. *Essai sur le gommier et le commerce de gomme dans les escales du Sénégal*. Dakar, 1963.

_____. *Histoire de la Mauritanie*. Nouakchott, 1964.

Diagne, Pathé. *Pouvoir politique traditionnel en Afrique occidentale*. Paris, 1967.

Dieterlen, G. "Mythe et organisation sociale au Soudan français." *Journal de la Société des africanistes*, 25:39-76 (1955) and 29:119-38 (1959).

Dixey, F. "Primitive Iron-Ore Smelting Methods in West Africa." *The Mining Magazine*, 23:213-16 (1920).

Dodwell, H. "Le Sénégal sous la domination anglaise." *RHCF*, 4:267-300 (1916).

Donnan, Elizabeth. *Documents Illustrative of the History of the Slave Trade to America*. 4 vols. Washington, D. C., 1930-35.

Doursther, Horace. *Dictionnaire universel des poids et mesures anciens et modernes*. 1840; reprint edition, Amsterdam, 1965.

Dubie, Paul. "La vie materielle des Maures." In *Melanges ethnologiques*. Dakar, 1953. Pp. 110-252. Mémoires de l'*IFAN*, no. 23.

Ducasse. "Mémoire ou relation du Sr. Ducasse sur son voyage de Guynée avec *La Tempeste* en 1687 et 1688." In Paul Roussier, *L'établissement d'Issiny, 1687-1702*. Paris, 1935.

Duchon-Doris, Jr., J. P. *Commerce des toiles bleues, dit Guinées*. Paris, 1842.

Duncan, T. Bentley. *Atlantic Islands: Madeira, the Azores, and the Cape Verdes in Seventeenth-Century Commerce and Navigation*. Chicago, 1972.

Dupire, Marguerite. "Trade and Markets in the Economy of the Nomadic Fulani of Niger (Bororo)." In P. Bohannan and G. Dalton, *Markets in Africa*. Evanston, 1962. Pp. 334-64.

_____. *Peuls nomades: Etude descriptive des Wodaabe du sahel nigérien*. Paris, Institut d'ethnologie, 1962.

_____. "Matériaux pour l'étude de l'endogamie des Peul du Cercle de Kédougou (Sénégal oriental)." *Bulletin et mémoires de la Société d'anthropologie de Paris*, 5 (11th series):223-98 (1963).

Durand, Jean Baptiste Léonard. *Voyage au Sénégal*. 2d ed. in 2 vols. Paris, 1807. First published, Paris, An X (Sept. 1802-Sept. 1803).

_____. *Atlas pour servir au voyage du Sénégal*. Paris, 1807.

Dwight, Theodore. "On the Sereculeh Nation, in Nigritia." *American Annals of Education and Instruction*, 5, 451-56 (1835).

Einzig, Paul. *Primitive Money*. London, 1949.

_____. *The History of Foreign Exchange*. New York, 1962.

Eisner, Gisela. *Jamaica, 1830-1930*. Manchester, 1961.

Emerit, Marcel. "Les liaisons terrestres entre le Soudan et l'Afrique du Nord au xviiie et au début du xixe siècle." *Travaux de l'Institut de recherches sahariennes*, 11:29-47 (1954).

Engerman, Stanley L., and Eugene D. Genovese, eds. *Race and Slavery in the Western Hemisphere: Quantitative Studies*. Princeton, 1974.

Epstein, T. Scarlett. *Capitalism, Primitive and Modern: Some Aspects of Tolai Economic Growth*. Canberra, 1968.

Equilbecq, Francois Victor. *Contes indigènes de l'ouest africain français*. 3 vols. Paris, 1913-16.

Faidherbe, Louis Léon César. "L'avenir du Sahara et du Soudan." *Revue maritime et coloniale*, 8:221-48 (1863).

_____. *Grammaire et vocabulaire de la langue Poul à l'usage des voyageurs dans le Soudan*. Paris, 1882.

_____. "Notice sur la colonie du Sénégal." *Annuaire du Sénégal et Dépendences*, 1858, pp. 71-144.

_____. "Populations noires du Sénégal et du Haut-Niger." *Bulletin de la Société de géographie de Paris*, 11 (4th series): 281-300 (1856).

_____. *Le Sénégal: La France dans l'Afrique occidentale*. Paris, 1889.

Faro, Jorge. "O movimento comercial do porto de Bissau de 1788 a 1794." *Boletim cultural da Guine Portugesa*, 14:231-58 (1959).

Faure, Claude. "Documents inédits sur l'histoire du Sénégal (1816-1822)." *Bulletin de la section de géographie, Comité des traveaux historiques et scientifiques*, 29:80-127 (1914-1916).

_____. "La garnison européene du Sénégal (1779-1858)." *RHCF*, 8:5-108 (1920).

_____. "Le premier séjour de Duranton au Sénégal (1819-1826). *RHCF*, 9:189-263 (1921).

_____. "Le voyage d'exploration de Grout de Beaufort au Senegal en 1824 et 1825. *Bulletin de la section de géographie, Comité des travaux historiques et scientifiques*, 34:146-204 (1919).

Fernandes, Valentin. *Description de la côte occidentale d'Afrique (Sénégal au Cap Monte, Archipels) par. V. Fernandes (1506-1510)*. Bissau, 1951.

Firth, Raymond, ed. *Themes in Economic Anthropology.* London, 1967.

_____, and B. S. Yamey, eds. *Capital, Saving and Credit in Peasant Societies: Studies from Asia, Oceania, the Caribbean, and Middle America.* London, 1964.

Fisher, Raymond. *The Russian Fur Trade, 1500-1700.* Berkeley, 1943.

Flize, Louis. "Le Bambouk." *Le Moniteur du Sénégal et dépendances* no. 51, pp. 3-4, and no. 52, p. 3 (17 and 24 March, 1857).

_____. "Le Boundou." *Moniteur du Sénégal,* no. 37, p. 2 (9 Dec. 1856).

_____. "Le Ndiambour et le Gadiaga (Provinces du Senegal)." *Revue coloniale,* 17 (2nd series):390-98 (1857).

_____. "Le Gadiaga." *Moniteur du Sénégal et dépendences,* no. 42, pp. 3-4 (Jan. 1857).

_____. "Le Boundou (Sénégal)." *Revue coloniale,* 17 (2nd series) 175-78 (1857).

_____. "Exploration dans le Bambouk (Sénégal)." *Revue coloniale,* 17 (2nd series):384-89 (1857).

_____. "Le Sénégal, le Niger, et le lac Tchad." *Revue coloniale,* 17 (2nd series):276-83 (1857).

Forbes, R. H. "The Black Man's Industries." *Geographical Review,* 23:230-47 (1933).

Ford, John. *The Role of Trypanosomiasis in African Ecology: A Study of the Tsetse Fly Problem.* Oxford, 1971.

Forêt, Auguste. *Un voyage dans le haut Sénégal.* Paris, 1888.

Fox, William. *A Brief History of the Wesleyan Missions on the Western Coast of Africa.* London, 1851.

France. Administration des Douanes. *Tableau général du commerce de la France avec les colonies et les puissances étrangères.* Paris, 1825-1895.

_____. Direction générale des Douanes. *Tableau décennal du commerce de la France. Volume I, 1837-46.* Paris, 1848.

_____. Ministère des colonies. *Statistiques coloniales.* Paris, 1832-   ).

Francis-Beuf, Claude. "L'industrie autochtone du fer en Afrique occidentale française." *CEHSAOF,* 20:403-64 (1937).

French West Africa. Comité d'études historiques et scientifiques de l'A.O.F. *Coutumiers juridiques de l'Afrique occidentale française,* 3 vols. Paris, 1939.

Froidveaux, Henri. "Une exploration oubliée de la Falémé (Voyage du Duliron en 1740." *Revue africaine,* 1905, pp. 192-97, 198-204

_____. "La découverte de la chute du Félou, 1687." *Bulletin de géographie historique et descriptive,* 13:300-321 (1898).

_____. "Une lettre d'Adanson pendant son voyage au Sénégal." *RHCF,* 5:79-90 (1917).

_____. "Les mémoires inédites d'Adanson sur l'Ile de Gorée et la Guyane française." *Bulletin de géographie historique et descriptive,* 14:76-100 (1899).

_____. "Le plan de colonisation du Senegal en 1802 (notes critiques)." *RHCF,* 7:177-94 (1919).

Gaden, Henri. "Du régime des terres de la vallée du Sénégal au Fouta antérieurement a l'occupation française." *Renseignements coloniaux*, no. 10, pp. 246-50 (1911). Republished in *CEHSAOF*, 18:403-14 (1935).

_____. "La gomme en Mauritanie." *Annales de l'académie des sciences coloniales*, 4:219-27 (1929).

_____. *Proverbes et maximes peules et toucouleurs, traduits, expliqués, et annotés*. Paris, 1931.

_____. "Légendes et coutumes sénégalaises: Cahiers de Yoro Dyao." *Revue d'ethnographie et de sociologie*, 3:119-137, 191-202 (1912).

Gaignat de Laulnais, C. F. *Guide de Commerce*. Paris, 1764.

Gamble, David P. *The Wolof of Senegambia*. London, 1957.

Gaudio, Attilio. *Les civilisations du Sahara*. Vervier, 1967.

Geertz, Clifford. *Peddlers and Princes: Social Change and Economic Modernization in Two Indonesian Towns*. Chicago, 1963.

[Geoffrey de Villeneuve, R.], R. G. V. *L'Afrique ou histoire, moeurs, usages, et coutumes des africains*. 4 vols. Paris, 1814.

Girard, J. "Note sur l'histoire traditionelle de la haute Casamance." *BIFAN*, 28:540-54 (1966).

Golberry, Sylvain Meinrad Xavier de. *Fragmens d'un voyage en Afrique, fait pendant les années 1785, 1786, 1787, dans les contrées occidentales de ce continent, comprises entres le cap Blanc de Barbarie . . . et le cap des palmes . . .* 2 vols. Paris, An X (1802).

Goody, Jack. *Technology, Tradition, and the State in Africa*. London, 1971.

Grant, Douglas. *The Fortunate Slave: An Illustration of African Slavery in the Early Eighteenth Century*. London, 1968.

Gravrand, Henri. *Visage africain de l'Eglise*. Paris, 1961.

Gray, John M. *History of the Gambia*. London, 1940.

Gray, Richard and David Birmingham, eds. *Pre-Colonial African Trade*. London, 1970.

Gray, William. *Travels in Western Africa in the Years 1818, 19, 20 and 21*. London, 1825.

Great Britain. Privy Council. *Report of the Lords of the Committee of Council for . . . Trade and Foreign Plantations . . . Concerning the Present State of Trade to Africa, and Particularly the Trade in Slaves . . .* London, 1789.

Grénier, Ph. "Les peuls du Ferlo." *Cahiers d'outre-mer*, 13:28-58 (1960).

Grout de Beaufort, E. "Extrait d'une lettre adressé à M. Jomard par M. de Beaufort, en mission dans le Sénégal." *Bulletin de la Société de geographie de Paris*, 3:332-33 (1825).

Guébhard, Paul. "Les Peulh du Fouta Dialon." *Revue des études ethnographiques et sociologiques*, 2:85-108 (1909).

_____. *Au Fouta-Djallon: Elevage, agriculture, commerce, régime foncier, religion*. Paris, 1910.

Guessin, Robert. "Introduction a l'étude du Sénégal oriental (Cercle de Kédougou)." *Bulletin de la Société d'anthropologie de Paris* (11th series):1-85 (supplementary volume for 1963).

Guèye, M'Baye. "La fin de l'esclavage à Saint-Louis et à Gorée en 1848." *BIFAN*, 28:637-56 (1966).

Hakluyt, Richard, ed. *The Principall Navigations Voiages*

and Discoveries of the English Nation, 2 vols. London, 1965.

Hallett, Robin. *The Penetration of Africa: European Exploration in North and West Africa to 1815.* New York, 1965.

_____, ed. *Records of the African Association.* London, 1964.

Hāmid, Ismā'il, ed. and trans. *Chroniques de la Mauritanie sénégalaise.* Paris, 1911.

Hardy, Georges. *La mise en valeur du Sénégal.* Paris, 1921.

_____. "L'affaire Duranton." *Annuaire et mémoires du comité d'études historiques et scientifiques de l'A. O. F.,* 2:413-36 (1917).

Hargreaves, John D. *West Africa: The Former French States.* Englewood Cliffs, New Jersey, 1967.

Haswell, M. R. *The Changing Pattern of Economic Activity in a Gambia Village.* London, 1963.

Hecquard, Louis Hyacinthe. "Rapport sur un voyage d'exploration dans l'intérieur de l'Afrique." *Nouvelles annales de la marine et des colonies,* 7:141-71 (1852).

_____. *Voyage sur la côte et dans l'intérieur de l'Afrique occidentale.* Paris, 1853.

Helm, June, Paul Bohannan, and Marshall D. Sahlins, eds. *Essays in Economic Anthropology.* Seattle, 1965.

Hertslet, Lewis. *The Map of Africa by Treaty.* 2d ed. in 3 vols. London, 1909.

_____. *A Complete Collection of the Treaties and Conventions, and Reciprocal Regulations . . . as far as they relate to Commerce and Navigation . . .* 30 vols. London, 1925.

Hiskett, M. "Materials relating to the Cowry Currency of the Western Sudan." *Bulletin of the School of Oriental and African Studies,* 29:122-42, 339-66 (1966).

Hodder, B. W., and Ukwu I. Ukwu. *Markets in West Africa: Studies in Markets and Trade Among the Yoruba and Ibo.* Ibadan, 1969.

Hodge, Carleton T., ed. *Papers on the Manding.* Bloomington, Ind., 1971.

Hodges, Cornelius, in Thora G. Stone, "The Journey of Cornelius Hodges in Senegambia." *English Historical Review,* 39:89-95 (1924).

Hopkins, A. G. "The Currency Revolution in South-West Nigeria in the Late Nineteenth Century," *JHSN,* 3:471-583 (1966).

Hopkins, Nicholas S. "Mandinka Social Organization." In Carleton T. Hodge, ed., *Papers on the Manding.* Bloomington, 1971. Pp. 99-128.

Horton, J. A. B. *West African Countries and Peoples.* London, 186

Houdas, O., [trans.]. *Tedzkiret en Nizian.* 2 vols. Paris, 1901.

Howard, Joseph Kinsey. *Strange Empire.* New York, 1952.

Hubert, Henry. "Coutumes indigènes en matière d'exploitation de gîtes aurifères en Afrique occidentale." *Annuaire et mémoires du comité d'études historiques et scientifiques de l'A.O.F.,* 2:226-43 (1917).

Idowu, H. A. "Café au Lait: Senegal's Mulatto Community in the Nineteenth Century." *Journal of the Historical Society of Nigeria,* 6:271-88 (1972).

Ingram. "Abridged Account of an Expedition of about Two Hundred Miles up the Gambia." *JRGS,* 17:150-55 (1847).

Irwin, John, and P. R. Schwartz. *Studies in Indo-European Textile History.* Ahmedabad, India: Calico Museum of Textile, 1966.

Jackson, J. F. *An Account of the Empire of Morocco.* London, 1811.

Jamburia, Omar. "The Story of the Gihad or Holy War of the Foulahs." *Sierra Leone Studies,* 3:30-34 (1919).

Janneguin, Claude, Sieur de Rochefort. *Voyage de Lybie au royaume de Sénéga, le long du Niger, avec la description des habitans qui sont le lon de ce fleuve, leurs coutumes et façon de vivre, les particularités les plus remarquable de ces pays.* Paris, 1643.

Jenkinson, H. "Records of the English African Companies." *Transactions of the Royal Historical Society,* 6 (3rd series): 185-220 (1912).

Jobson, Richard. *The Golden Trade, or a Discovery of the River Gambia* . . . London, 1932. First published 1623.

Johnson, Marion. "Cowrie Currencies of West Africa." *JAH,* 11: 17-49, 331-53 (1970).

_____. "The Nineteenth-Century Gold 'Mithqal' in West and North Africa." *JAH,* 9:547-69 (1968).

_____. "The Ounce in Eighteenth-Century West African Trade." *JAH,* 7:197-214 (1966).

Jomard, E. F. "Notice sur feu M. de Beaufort, voyageur en Afrique, lue à l'Association générale de la Société de géographie, le 31 mars 1826." *Bulletin de la Sociéte de géographie de Paris,* 5 (1st series):600-610 (1826).

_____. "Remarques géographiques sur les parties inférieures du cours du Sénégal et de celui de la Gambie, accompagnées de deux cartes et d'une note sur les positions de Tombouctou et de Ségo." *Bulletin de la Société de géographie de Paris,* 10:16-35 (1828).

Jones, G. I. "Native and Trade Currencies in Southern Nigeria during the Eighteenth and Nineteenth Centuries." *Africa,* 28: 43-54 (1958).

_____. *The Trading States of the Oil Rivers.* London, 1963.

Jore, Léonce. "Les établissements français sur la côte occidentale d'Afrique de 1758 à 1809." *RFHC,* 51:3-477 (1964).

Joucla, Edmond A. *Bibliographie de l'Afrique occidentale française.* Paris, 1937.

Kaké, Baba Ibrahima. "L'aventure des Bukhara (prétoriens noirs) au Maroc au xviiie siècle." *Présence africaine,* 70:67-74 (1969).

Kamara, Cheikh Moussa. "La vie d'el-Hadji Omar." Translated and edited by Amar Samb. *BIFAN* (series B), 32:44-135, 370-411, 770-818.

Kane, Abdou Salam. "Du régime des terres chez les populations du Fouta sénégalais." *CEHSAOF,* 18:449-61 (1935).

Kane, Abdoulaye. "Histoire et origine des familles du Fouta-Toro." *Annuaire de la comité d'études historiques et scientifiques de l'A.O.F.,* 1:325-43 (1916).

Kane, Oumar. "Samba Gelajo-Jegi." *BIFAN,* 32:911-26 (1970).

Kâti, Mahmoûd ben El-Hâdj. *Tarikh El-Fettach.* Translated by O. Houdas and M. Delafosse. Paris, 1964.

Kea, R. A. "Firearms and Warfare on the Gold and Slave Coasts from the Sixteenth to the Nineteenth Centuries." *JAH*, 12:185-213 (1971).

Kirk-Greene, A. H. M. "The Major Currencies in Nigerian History." *JHSN*, 2:132-50 (1960).

Klein, Martin. *Islam and Imperialism in Senegal: Sine-Saloum, 1847-1914.* Stanford, 1968.

Knight-Baylac, Marie Hélène. "La vie à Gorée de 1677 à 1789." *RHCF*, 58:377-420 (1970).

Labarthe, Pierre. *Voyage en Sénégal pendant les années 1784 et 1785, d'après les mémoires de Lajaille.* Paris, 1802.

Labat, Jean Baptiste. *Nouvelle relation de l'Afrique occidentale.* 4 vols. Paris, 1728.

Labouret, Henri. *La langue des Peuls ou Foulbé.* Dakar, *IFAN*, 1952.

_____. *La langue des Peuls ou Foulbé: Lexique français-peul.* Dakar, *IFAN*, 1955.

Labouret, Henri, Jean Canu, Jean Fournier, and Georges Bonmarchand. *Le commerce extra-européene jusqu'aux temps modernes.* Paris, 1953.

Labrousse, C. E. *Esquisse du mouvement des prix et des revenus en France au xviiie siècle.* 2 vols. Paris, 1933.

La Chapelle, F. de. "Esquisse d'une histoire du Sahara occidental." *Hésperis*, 11:35-95 (1930).

La Courbe. *Premier voyage du Sieur de la Courbe fait à la coste d'Afrique en 1685.* Edited by Pierre Cultru. Paris, 1913.

Lacroix, Louis. *Les derniers négriers.* Paris, 1952.

Ladurantie et Durécu. *Résponse des SS. Ladurantie et Durécu, négocians de Bordeaux, a l'écrit calomnieux publié sous le nom de mémoire pour le Colonel Laserre, Ex-commandant du Sénégal.* Paris, 1805.

Lamartiny, J. J. *Etudes africaines: Le Bondou et le Bambouc.* Paris, 1884.

Lambert, A. "Voyage dans le Fouta-Djalon, côtes occidentales d'Afrique (février-juin 1860)." *Revue maritime et coloniale,* 2:1-51 (1861).

Lambrecht, Frank L. "Aspects of Evolution and Ecology of Tse-tse Flies and Trypanosomiasis in Prehistoric African Environment." *JAH*, 5:1-24 (1964).

Lamiral, Dominique Harcourt. *L'Affrique et le peuple affriquain.* Paris, 1789.

_____. *Mémoire sur le Sénégal.* Paris, 1791.

Lampard, Eric E. "The Price System and Economic Change: A Commentary on Theory and History." *Journal of Economic History*, 20:617-37 (1960).

_____. "Historical Aspects of Urbanization." In P. M. Hauser and L. F. Schnore, eds., *The Study of Urbanization.* New York, 1965. Pp. 519-54.

Lancaster, Lorraine. "Crédit épargne et investissement dans une économie 'non-monetaire'." *Archives européenes de sociologie,* 3:149-64 (1962).

Landes, David S. *The Unbound Prometheus: Technological Change and Industrial Development in Western Europe from 1750 to the Present.* Cambridge, 1969.

Lane, Frederic C. "Tonnages, Medieval and Modern." *Economic History Review*, 17 (2nd series):213-33 (1964).

Lanrezac, [Victor L. M.] "Légendes soudanaises." *Revue économique française*, 5:607-19 (1907).

Lasnet, Dr. "Les races du Sénégal." In Lasnet and others, *Une mission au Sénégal*. Paris, 1900. Pp. 1-193.

_____, A. Chevalier, A. Cigny, and P. Rambaud. *Une mission au Sénégal*. Paris, 1900.

Lasserre, Guy. "L'or du Soudan." *Cahiers d'outre-mer*, 1:368-74 (1948).

Lawrence, Arnold W. *Trade Castles and Forts of West Africa*. Stanford, 1964.

Leblanc. "Voyage à Galam en 1820." *Annales maritimes et coloniales*, part 2, vol. 1, for 1822. Pp. 133-159.

LeClair, Edward E., Jr. "Economic Theory and Economic Anthropology." *American Anthropologist*, 64:1179-1203 (1962).

LeClair, Edward E., Jr., and Harold K. Schneider. *Economic Anthropology: Readings in Theory and Analysis*. New York, 1968.

Leeds, Anthony. "The Port-of-Trade in Pre-European India as an Ecological and Evolutionary Type." *Proceedings of the 1961 Annual Spring Meeting of the American Ethnological Society*. Seattle, Washington, 1961. Pp. 26-48.

Leger, Marcel and L. Teppaz. "Le 'Horse-Sickness' au Sénégal et au Soudan français." *CEHSAOF*, 5:219-40 (1922).

Legrand, Réné. "Le Fouladou." *La géographie*, 24:241-53 (1912).

Lejean, Guillavine. "Le Sénégal en 1859 et les routes commerciales du Sahara." *Revue contemporaine*, 11:368-403 (1859).

LeMaire, Jacques-Joseph. *Voyage to the Canaries, Cape Verd, and the Coast of Africa under the command of M. Dancourt (1682)*. Translated by Edmund Goldsmid. Edinburgh, 1887.

Lemos, Coelho. *See* Coelho, Francisco de Lemos.

Leriche, A. "Anthroponymie toucouleur." *BIFAN*, 18:169-88, 1-2 (1956).

_____. "Notes sur les classes sociales et sur quelque tribus de Mauritanie." *BIFAN*, 17:173-203 (1955).

_____, and Mokhtar ould Hamidoun. "Notes sur le Trarza: Essai de géographie historique." *BIFAN*, 10:461-538 (1948).

[Lespinot]. "Sénégal. Saint Louis. Esclavage des nègres dans l'établissement français." *Revue encyclopédique*, 37:549-51 (1828).

Lestrange, Monique de. *Les Coniagui et les Bassari*. Paris, 1955.

Levtzion, Nehemia. *Muslims and Chiefs in West Africa*. Oxford, 1968.

Lindsay, Rev. John. *A Voyage to the Coast of Africa in 1758*. London, 1759.

Ling Roth, Henry. "Studies in Primitive Looms." *Journal of the Royal Anthropological Institute*, 46:285-308; 47:113-50; 48:103-45 (1916-18).

Lintingre, Pierre. *Voyage du Sieur de Glicourt à la côte occidentale d'Afrique pendant les années 1778 et 1779*. Dakar, 1966.

L'Orza de Reichenberg. "De Kayes au Bambouk." *Revue de géographie*, 30:101-12, 161-71 (1892).

Ly, Abdoulaye. *La Compagnie du Sénégal*. Paris, 1958.

_____. "Conséquences des cas Labat et Loyer." *BIFAN*, 15:751-66 (1953).

Ly, Djibril. "Coutumes et contes des Toucouleurs du Fouta Toro." *CEHSAOF*, 21:304-26 (1938).

Macbriar, R. Maxwell. *Sketches of a Missionary's Travels in Egypt, Syria, Western Africa, etc.* London, 1839.

Machat, J. *Documents sur les établissements français et l'Afrique occidentale au xviiie siècle*. Paris, 1906.

Macklin, R. "Queens and Kings of Niumi." *Man*, 35:67-68 (1935).

Magalhães-Godinho, Vitorino. *L'économie de l'empire portugais aux xve et xvie siècles*. Paris, 1969.

Mahoney, Florence K. Omolara. "Notes on Mulattoes of the Gambia Before the Mid-Nineteenth Century. *Transactions of the Historical Society of Ghana*, 8:120-29 (1966).

Makarius, Laura. "Observations sur la légende des griots malinké." *CEA*, 9:626-40 (1969).

Marche, Alfred. *Trois voyages en Afrique occidentale*. 2nd ed. Paris, 1882.

Marmol Carvajal, Luis del. *La descripción general de Affrica, con todos los successos de guerras que a avido . . . hasta el año del señor 1751*. 3 vols. Granada and Málaga, 1573-99.

Martin, Eveline C. *The British West African Settlements 1750-1821*. London, 1927.

Martin, Gaston. *Histoire de l'esclavage dans les colonies françaises*. Paris, 1948.

_____. *Nantes au xviiie siècle: L'ère des négriers (1714-1774)*. Paris, 1931.

Marty, Paul. "Cheikh Sidïa et sa voie (Mauritanie)." *RMM*, 31:29-133 (1915-16).

_____. *Etudes sur Islam en Sénégal*. 2 vols. Paris, 1917.

_____. *Etudes sur l'Islam et les tribus Maures, les Brakna*. Paris, 1921.

_____. *Etudes sénégalaises*. Paris, n.d. [c. 1926].

_____, [trans.]. "Les chroniques de Oualata et de Néma." *Revue des études islamique*, 1:355-426, 531-75 (1927).

_____. "Les groupements Tidianïa derivés d'al-Hadj Omar." *RMM*, 31:221-364 (1915-16).

_____. "Les Ida ou Ali, chorfa Tidiania de Mauritanie." *RMM*, 31:223-73 (1915-16).

_____. *L'Islam en Guinée*. Paris, 1921.

_____. *L'émirat des Trarzas*. Paris, 1919.

_____. "Tableau historique de Cheikh Sidia." *CEHSAOF*, 4:76-95 (1921).

Masson, Paul. "Une double énigme: André Brue." *RHCF*, 25:9-34 (193

Mauny, Raymond. "La monnaie marginelloïde de l'ouest africain." *BIFAN*, 15:659-69 (1957).

_____. *Tableau géographique de l'ouest africain au moyen age*. Dakar, 1961.

Mauro, Frédéric. *Le Portugal et l'Atlantique au xviie siècle (1570-1670): Etude économique*. Paris, 1960.

Mbaeyi, P. M. "The British-Barra War of 1831: A Reconsideration
of its Origins and Importance." *JHSN*, 3:617-31 (June, 1967).

McCall, Daniel F. "The Cultural Map and Time-Profile of the Mande-
Speaking Peoples." In Carleton T. Hodge, ed., *Papers on the
Manding*. Bloomington, Ind., 1971. Pp. 27-98.

McManus, John C. "An Economic Analysis of Indian Behavior in the
North American Fur Trade." *The Journal of Economic History*,
32:36-53 (1972).

Meilink-Roelofsz, M. A. P. *Asian Trade and European Influence
in the Indonesian Archipelago Between 1500 and 1630*. The Hague,
1962.

Meillassoux, Claude. *De l'économie d'auto-subsistance à l'agriculture commerciale en pays gouro (Côte d'Ivoire)*. Paris-La
Haye, 1964.

_____. "Essai d'interpretation du phénomène économique dans
les sociétés traditionnelles et d'auto-subsistance." *CEA*, 1:
38-67 (1960).

_____. "Histoire et institutions du *kafo* de Bamako d'après la
tradition des Niaré." *CEA*, 4:186-227 (1963).

_____, ed. *The Development of Indigenous Trade and Markets in
West Africa*. London, 1971.

_____, Lassana Doucouré, and Diaowé Simgha. *Légende de la dis-
persion des Kusa (Epopée Soninke)*. Dakar, 1967.

Meniaud, Jacques. *Haut-Sénégal-Niger: Géographie économique*.
2 vols. Paris, 1912.

Mercier, Roger. *L'Afrique noire dans la littérature française:
Les premières images (17e-18e siècles)*. Dakar, 1962.

Mère, G. "Les salines du Trarza." *Renseignements coloniaux*,
7:161-67 (1911).

Miské, Ahmed Baba. "Al Wasît: Tableau de la Mauritanie à la fin
du xixe siècle." *BIFAN*, 30:117-64 (1968).

Mollien, Gaspard Theodore. *Travels in the Interior of Africa*.
Translated from the French by T. E. Bowdich. London, 1820.

Monserat. "Mémoire inédite de Monserat sur l'histoire du Nord du
Sénégal de 1819 à 1839." Annotated and presented by Boubacar
Barry. *BIFAN*, series B, 32:1-43 (1970).

Monteil, Charles. *Contes soudanais*. Paris, 1905.

_____. *Djenné*. Paris, 1932.

_____. "Fin de siècle à Médine (1898-1899)." *BIFAN*, 28:84-171
(1966).

_____. "La légende du Ouagadou et l'origine du Soninké."
Mélanges ethnologiques. Dakar, 1953.

_____. "Le coton chez les noirs." *CEHSAOF*, 11:585-684 (1926).

_____. *Les Khassonké*. Paris, 1915.

_____. "Le site de Goundiourou." *CEHSAOF*, 11:647-53 (1928).

_____. "Le Tékrour et la Guinée." *Outre-Mer*, 1:387-405 (1929).

_____. "Reflexions sur le problème des Peuls." *Journal de la
Société des africanistes*, 20:153-92 (1950).

Monteil, Vincent. *Esquisses sénégalaises*. Dakar, 1966.

_____. "Goundiourou." *Notes africaines*, 12:63-64 (1941).

_____. "Le Dyolof et Al-Bouri Ndiaye." *BIFAN*, 28:595-636 (1966).

Monteilhet, J. "Documents relatifs à l'histoire du Sénégal."
CEHSAOF, 1:62-119 (1916).

_____. "Le duc de Lauzun, gouverneur du Sénégal." *CEHSAOF*, 3: 193-237, 515-63 (1920).

_____. "Les finances et commerce du Sénégal pendant les guerres de la Révolution et de l'Empire." *CEHSAOF*, 2:362-412 (1917).

Moore, Francis. *Travels into the Inland Parts of Africa* . . . London, 1738.

Moraes, Nize Izabel de. "Sur les prises de Gorée par les Portugais au xviie siècle." *BIFAN*, 31:989-1013 (1969).

Moreira, J. M. "Os Fulas da Guiné portuguesa na panorâmica geral do mundo fula." *Boletim cultural da Guiné portuguesa*, 19:289-327, 417-32 (1964).

Morenas, J. *Pétition contre la traite des noirs qui se fait au Sénégal*. Paris, 1820.

_____. *Précis historique de la traite des noirs et de l'esclavage colonial*. Paris, 1828.

Morgan, W. B., and J. C. Pugh. *West Africa*. London, 1969.

Morse, Richard M., ed. *The Bandeirantes*. New York, 1965.

Mouette, Germain. *Histoire des conquests de Mouley Archy, connu sous le nom de roy de Tafilet, et de Mouley Ismaël ou Seméin* . . . Paris, 1683. Reprinted as "Historie de Moylay er-Rechid et de Moulay Ismail," in Henri, comte de Castries, *Sources inédite de l'histoire du Maroc de 1580 à 1845*, 2 (2nd series):1-199.

Muhammad al-Saghôr ibn al-Hâjj Muhammad al-Wufrânî. *Histoire de la dynastie saadienne au Maroc*. Translated by O. Houdas from Mozhet el-Hâdi. Paris, 1888-89.

Nardin, Jean Claude. "Recherches sur les 'gourmets' d'Afrique occidentale." *RHFC*, 53:215-44 (1966).

Neale, Walter C. "On Defining 'Labor' and 'Services' for Comparative Studies." *American Anthropologist*, 66:1300-1307 (1964).

Neild, Alderman. "An Account of the Price of Printing Cloth and Upland Cotton from 1812 to 1860 A.D." *Journal of the Royal Statistical Society*, 24:491-97 (1861).

Newbury, Colin W., ed. *British Policy toward West Africa: Select Documents, 1786-1914*. 2 vols. Oxford, 1965-71.

_____. "Credit in Early Nineteenth-Century West African Trade." *JAH*, 13:81-95 (1972).

_____. "Trade and Authority in West Africa from 1850 to 1880." In L. H. Gann and Peter Duignan, eds., *Colonialism in Africa*. 4 vols. to date. Cambridge, 1967- . Vol. 1, pp. 66-99.

_____. "North African and Western Sudan Trade in the Nineteenth Century: A Re-evaluation." *JAH*, 7:233-46 (1966).

Niane, Djibril Tamsir. "A propos de Koli Tenguella." *Recherches africaines*, 4:33-36 (1960).

Noirot, Ernest. *A travers le Fouta-Djallon et le Bambouck*. Paris, 1882.

Norris, H. T. "Znãga Islam during the Seventeenth and Eighteenth Centuries." *Bulletin of the School of Oriental and African Studies*, 32:496-526 (1969).

North, Douglas. "Ocean Freight Rates and Economic Development, 1750-1913." *Journal of Economic History*, 18:537-55 (1958).

_____. "Sources of Productivity Change in Ocean Shipping, 1600-1850." *Journal of Political Economy*, 76:953-70 (1968).

Ogilby, John. *Africa*. London, 1670.

Ogot, B. A., and J. A. Kieran, eds. *Zamani: A Survey of East African History*. Nairobi, 1968.

Pacheco Pereira, Duarte. *Esmeraldo de Situ Orbis*. Edited by Raymond Mauny. Bissau, 1956.

Pageard, Robert. "Contribution critique à la chronologie historique de l'Ouest africain." *Journal de la Société des africanistes*, 32:91-177 (1962).

_____. "Un mystérieux voyage au pays de Bambouc (1789)." *Notes africaines*, no. 1, pp. 23-27 (January, 1961).

Pales, Léon. *Les sels alimentaires. Sels minéraux. Problème des sels alimentaires en A.O.F.* Dakar, 1950.

Park, Mungo. *Travels in the Interior Districts of Africa*. 2 vols. London, 1816-17.

Pascal, S. L. "Voyage au Bambouk et retour à Bakel." In *La tour du monde*, 3:39-48 (1861).

_____. "Voyage d'exploration dans le Bambouk, Haut-Sénégal." *Revue algérienne et coloniale*, 3:137-64 (1860).

Pasquier, Roger. "A propos de l'émancipation des esclaves au Sénégal en 1848." *RFHC*, 54:188-208 (1968).

_____. "Villes du Sénégal au xixᵉ siècle." *RHCF*, 47:387-426 (1960).

Patenostre, Dr. "La captivité chez les peuples du Fouta-Djallon." *Outre-Mer*, 2:241-54, 353-72 (1930).

Pélissier, Paul. *Les paysans du Sénégal: Les civilisations agraires du Cayor à la Casamance*. St.-Yrieix, 1966.

Pelletan, Jean-Gabriel. *Mémoire sur la colonie française du Sénégal, avec quelque considérations historiques et politiques sur la traite des Nègres . . .* Edited by Marc-François Guillois. Paris, An XI.

Pellow, Thomas. *The Adventures of Thomas Pellow, of Penryn, Mariner*. Edited by Robert Brown. London, 1890. First published in 1740.

Person, Yves. "Les ancêtres de Samori." *CEA*, 4:125-56.

_____. *Samori: Une révolution Dyoula*. 2 vols. to date. Dakar, 1968- .

Polanyi, Karl. *Dahomey and the Slave Trade: An Analysis of an Archaic Economy*. Seattle, 1966.

_____. "Ports of Trade in Early Societies." *Journal of Economic History*, 23:30-45 (March 1963).

_____. *Primitive, Archaic and Modern Economies: Essays by Karl Polanyi*. Edited by George Dalton. New York, 1968.

_____. "Sortings and the 'Ounce Trade' in the West African Slave Coast." *JAH*, 5:331-93 (1964).

Polanyi, Karl, C. M. Arensberg, and H. W. Pearson. *Trade and Markets in the Early Empires*. Glencoe, 1957.

Pollet, Eric, and Grace Winter. *La société Soninké (Dyahunu, Mali)*. Brussels, 1972.

Pollet, Grace. "Bibliographie des Sarakolé." *Journal de la Société des africanistes*, 34:283-92.(1964).

Poole, Thomas Eyre. *Life, Scenery, and Customs in Sierra Leone and the Gambia*. 2 vols. London, 1850.

Porgès, Laurence. *Bibliographie des régions du Sénégal*. Dakar, Ministre du Plan et Dévelopment, 1967.

Portères, Roland. "La monnaie de fer dans l'ouest africain au xxe siècle." *Journal d'agriculture tropicale et de botanique appliquée*, 7:97-109 (1960).

Posthumus, Nicolaas Wilhelmus. *Inquiry into the History of Prices in Holland*. 2 vols. Leiden, 1946-64.

Postlethwayt, Malachy. *The Universal Dictionary of Trade and Commerce . . .* 2 vols. London, 1751.

Prélong. "Mémoires sur les iles de Gorée et du Sénégal." *Annales de chimie*, 18:241-303 (1793).

Prévost d'Exiles, Abbé Antoine-François. *Histoire générale des voyages*. New ed. in 25 vols. The Hague, 1747-80.

[Pruneau de Pommegorge, Antoine E.]. *Description de la Nigritie*. Amsterdam, 1789.

Quiggin, A. Hingston. *A Survey of Primitive Money*. London, 1949.

Quimby, George Irving. *Indian Culture and European Trade Goods: The Archaeology of the Historic Period in the Western Great Lakes Region*. Madison, 1966.

Quinn, Charlotte A. *Mandingo Kingdoms of the Senegambia: Traditionalism, Islam, and European Expansion*. London, 1972.

_____. "Niumi: A Nineteenth-Century Mandingo Kingdom." *Africa*, 38:443-55 (1968).

Raffenel, Anne. "Divers itinéraires de la Sénégambie et du Soudan." *Bulletin de la Société de géographie de Paris*, 12 (3rd series): 303-30 (1849).

_____. "Divers itinéraires de la Sénégambie et du Soudan, pour servir à l'intelligence de la carte ce-contre." *Revue coloniale*, 3 (2nd series):277-305 (1849).

_____. "Le Haut Sénégal et la Gambie en 1843 et 1844." *Revue coloniale*, 8:309-40 (1846).

_____. *Nouveau voyage au pays des nègres*. 2 vols. Paris, 1856.

_____. *Rapport sur le pays de Galam, le Bondou et le Bambouk, adressé le 17 mars 1844 au gouverneur du Sénégal*. Paris, 1844. Also published in *Moniteur universelle* and in *Revue coloniale*, 4:1-22, 136-218 (1844).

_____. "Second voyage d'exploration dans l'intérieur de l'Afriqu *Revue coloniale*, 13:1-47 (1847).

_____. "Second voyage d'exploration dans l'intérieur de l'Afriqu enterprise par M. A. Raffenel." *Revue coloniale*, 3 (2nd series): 217-76 (1849).

_____. *Voyage dans l'Afrique occidentale exécuté en 1843 et 1844* (Paris, 1846).

Rambert, Gaston, ed. *L'histoire du commerce de Marseille*. 7 vols. Paris, 1949-66.

Rançon, André. *Dans la haute Gambie: Voyage d'exploration scientifique 1891-92*. Paris, 1894.

_____. "Le Bondou." *Bulletin de la Société de géographie de Bordeaux*, 7 (new series):433-63, 465-84, 497-548, 561-91, 593-647 (1894).

Raybaud, Léon-Pierre. "L'administration du Sénégal de 1781 à 1784: L'affaire Dumontet." *Annales africaines*, 1968, pp. 113-72.

Rinchon, Dieudonné. *Le trafic négrier d'après les livres de commerce du capitaine gantois Pierre-Ignace-Liévin Van Alstein*. Vol. 1. Paris, 1938.

_____. *Pierre-Ignace-Liévin Van Alstein, capitaine négrier.*
Dakar, 1964.

Roberts, George [pseud.]. *Four Years of Voyages of Capt. George
Roberts . . .* London, 1726.

Robinson, David. "Abdul Qader and Shaykh Umar: A Continuing
Tradition of Islamic Leadership in Futa Toro." *International
Journal of African Historical Studies,* 6:386-403 (1973).

Robinson, David, Philip D. Curtin, and James P. Johnson. "A
Tentative Chronology of Fuuta Tooro from the Sixteenth through
the Nineteenth Centuries." *CEA,* 12:555-92 (1972).

Rodney, Walter. "Portuguese Attempts at Monopoly on the Upper
Guinea Coast, 1580-1650. *JAH,* 6:307-22 (1965).

_____. *A History of the Upper Guinea Coast 1545-1800.* Oxford,
1970.

_____. "Jihad and Social Revolution in Futa Djalon in the Eight-
eenth Century." *JHSN,* 4:269-84 (1968).

Roger, M. le baron. "Lettre de M. Roger, Gouverneur du Sénégal,
à M. Jomard, membre de la Société de géographie." *Bulletin
de la Société de géographie,* 2 (2nd series):176-78 (1824).

_____. "Résultats de questions adressées au nommé Mbouia,
marabou maure, de Tischit, et a un nègre de Walet, qui l'accom-
pagnait." *Recueil de voyages et de mémoires publié par la
Société de géographie.* Paris, 1825. Pp. 51-62.

Roubaud, Emile. "Les mouches tse-tses en Afrique occidentale
française." *CEHSAOF,* 3:257-300 (1920).

Roux, Emile. *Notice historique sur le Boundou.* Saint Louis,
1893.

Rouzée, P. "Itinéraire suivi par Hadji Boubeker, africain, de
Séno-Palel, ville de Fouta, à la Mecque." *Annales maritimes
et coloniales,* 1820 (2), pp. 937-45.

Ruiters, Dierick, G. Thilmans, and J. P. Rossie. "Le 'Flambeau
de la Navigation' de Dierick Ruiters." *BIFAN,* 31:106-19 (1969).

Ryder, Alan F. C. *Benin and the Europeans 1485-1897.* London, 1969.

Sahlins, M. D. "On the Sociology of Primitive Exchange." In M.
Banton, ed., *The Relevance of Models for Social Anthropology.*
Garden City, New York, 1967.

Saint-Père, Jules Hubert. *Les Sarakollé du Guidimakha.* Paris,
1925.

Sanson, d'Abbeville, Nicolas. *L'Affrique, en plusieurs cartes
nouvelles et exactes.* Paris, 1656.

Sasoon, Hamo. "Early Sources of Iron in Africa." *South African
Archaeological Bulletin,* 18:176-80 (1963).

Saugnier. *Relations de plusieurs voyages à la côte d'Afrique
à Maroc, au Sénégal, à Gorée, à Galam . . .* Paris, 1791.

Saulnier, Eugène. *La compagnie de Galam au Sénégal.* Paris, 1921.

Savary des Brulons, Jacques, and Philémont Louis Savary. *Le
parfait négociant.* 2 vols. Paris, 1777.

Savigny, J. B., and A. Correard. *Narrative of a Voyage to Senegal in 1816.* London, 1968.

Schnapper, Bernard. *La politique et le commerce français dans
le golfe de Guinée de 1838 à 1871.* Paris, 1961.

Schumpeter, Elizabeth. *English Overseas Trade Statistics, 1697-
1808.* Oxford, 1960.

140   Bibliography

Sénégal. *Bulletin administratif du Sénégal*. 1819-42.
Shefer, Christian, ed. *Instructions générales données de 1763
à 1870 aux gouverneurs et ordonnateurs des établissements
français en Afrique occidentale*. 2 vols. Paris, 1921.
Sidibé, M. "Fabrication du salpêtre ou nitrate de potassium et
de la poudre de chasse dans la région de Kita (Soudan français)."
Notes africaines, 24:23-24 (1944).
Silla, Ousmane. "Essai historique sur Portudal." *Notes afri-
caines*, 123:77-89 (1969).
Simmons, William Scranton. "Social organization among the
Badyaranke of Tonghia." *Cahiers du centre de recherches
anthropologiques*, 2 (12th series) 59-95 (1967).
_____. *Eyes of the Night: Witchcraft among a Senegalese People*.
Boston, 1971.
Sleen, W. G. N. van uer. "A Bead Factory in Amsterdam in the
Seventeenth Century." *Man*, 63:172-74 (1963).
Smelser, Neil. "A Comparative View of Exchange Systems."
Economic Development and Cultural Change, 7:173-82 (1959).
Smith, H. F. C. "A Neglected Theme of West African History: The
Islamic Revolutions of the 19th Century." *JHSN*, 2:169-85
(1961).
Smith, Michael G. "Exchange and Marketing among the Hausa." In
Bohannan and Dalton, *Markets in Africa*, pp. 299-334.
Smith, Pierre. "Notes sur l'organisation sociale des Diakhanke:
Aspects particuliers à la région de Kédougou." *Bulletin et
mémoires de la Société d'anthropologie de Paris*, 8 (11th series):
263-302 (1965) and 231-62 (1968).
_____. "Les Diakhanké: Histoire d'une dispersion." *Bulletin
et mémoires de la Société d'anthropologie de Paris*, 8 (11th
series):231-62 (1968).
Smith, Robert. "The Canoe in West African History." *JAH*, 11:
515-33 (1970).
Smith, William. *A New Voyage to Guinea*. London, 1744.
Soh, Siré Abbas. *Chroniques du Fouta sénégalais*. Translated,
annotated, and introduced by Maurice Delafosse and Henri Gaden.
Paris, 1913.
Sow, Alfâ Ibrâhîm. *Chroniques et récits du Foûta Djalon*. Paris,
1968.
_____. *Le femme, la vache, et la foi*. Paris, 1966.
Stenning, Derrick J. *Savannah Nomads*. London, 1959.
Stewart, Charles C., and E. K. *Islam and Social Order in Mauri-
tania: A Case Study from the Nineteenth Century*. Oxford, 1973.
Stibbs, Bartholomew, Edward Drummond, and Richard Hull. "Journal
of a Voyage up the Gambia." In Francis Moore, *Travels into the
Inland Parts of Africa*. London, 1738. Pp. 235-97.
Stucklé, Henri. *Le commerce de la France avec le Soudan*. Paris,
1864.
Sundström, Lars. *The Trade of Guinea*. Upsala, 1965.
Suret-Canale, Jean. "Touba in Guinea—Holy Place of Islam." In
Christopher Allen and R. W. Johnson, eds., *African Perspectives:
Papers in the History, Politics, and Economics of Africa Pre-
sented to Thomas Hodgkin*. Cambridge, 1970, pp. 53-81.
Sylla, Assane. "Une république africaine au xixe siècle (1795-

1857)." *Présence africaine*, nos. 1-2 (new series), pp. 47-65 (April-June 1955).

Szereszewski, Robert. *Structural Changes in the Economy of Ghana 1891-1911.* London, 1965.

Tardif, Jean. "Kédougou: Aspects de l'histoire de la situation socio-economique actuelle." *Bulletins et mémoires de la Société d'anthropologie de Paris,* 8 (11th series):167-230 (1965).

Tardits, Claudine and Claude. "Traditional Market Economy in South Dahomey." In Bohannan and Dalton, *Markets in Africa,* pp. 89-102.

Tautin, L. "Études critiques sur l'ethnologie et l'ethnographie des peuples du Bassin du Sénégal." *Revue ethnographique,* 4: 61-80, 137-47, 256-68 (1885).

Tauxier, Louis. *Histoire des Bambara.* Paris, 1942.

Techer, H. "Coutumes des Tendas." *CEHSAOF,* 16:630-66 (1933).

Teixeira da Mota, A. *Guiné portuguesa.* 2 vols. Lisboa, 1954.

_____. "D. João Bemoim e a expedição portuguesa ao Senegal em 1489." *Boletim cultural da Guiné portuguesa,* 26:63-111 (1971).

Teppaz, Louis. *Contribution à l'étude de la horse-sickness au Sénégal.* Paris, 1931.

Thaly, J. H. F. "Essai de topographie médicale du Haut-Sénégal." *Archives de la medecine navale,* 7:161-79, 349-64; 8:174-93 (1867).

Thilmans, Guy. "Sur l'existence, fin xvie, de comptoirs néer-landais à Joal et Portudal (Sénégal)." *Notes africaines,* 117: 17-19 (1968).

_____, and Nize Isabel de Moraes. "Le routier de la côte de Guinée de Francisco Pirez de Carvalho (1635)." *BIFAN,* 32:23-369 (1970).

Thurnwald, Richard. *Economics in Primitive Communities.* London, 1932.

Tooke, Thomas. *A History of Prices and of the State of Circulation from 1792 to 1856.* 6 vols. New York, 1928. First published 1838-57.

Toupet, Charles. "Orientation bibliographique sur la Mauritanie." *BIFAN,* 31:201-39 (1959) and 34:594-627 (1962).

Trimmingham, J. Spencer. *A History of Islam in West Africa.* Glasgow, 1962.

Trochain, Jean. *Contribution à l'étude de la végétation du Sénégal.* Paris, 1940.

Tyam, Mahmmadou Aliou. *La vie d'el Hadj Omar.* (Paris, 1935). Transcription by H. Gaden.

Vidal, M. "Etude sur la tenure des terres indigènes au Fouta." *CEHSAOF,* 18:415-48 (1935).

Vieillard, Gilbert Pierre. *Notes sur les coutumes des Peuls au Fouta-Djallon.* Paris, 1939.

Villault, Nicolas, Sieur de Bellefond. *Relations des costes d'Afrique appellées Guinée.* Paris, 1669.

Walckenaer, Charles A. [ed.] *Histoire générale des voyages.* 21 vols. Paris, 1826-31.

Wane, Yaya. *Les Toucouleur du Fouta Tooro (Sénégal): Strati-fication sociale et structure familiale.* Dakar, 1969.

_____. "Etat actuel de la documentation au sujet des Toucou-leurs." *BIFAN,* 25:459-77 (1963).

142   Bibliography

Warden, Alex J. *The Linen Trade, Ancient and Modern*. London,
    1864.
Washington, Captain [John]. "Some Account of Mohammedu-Sise,
    a Mandingo of Nyani-Maru on the Gambia." *JRGS*, 8:448-54.
Weber, Henry. *La compagnie française des Indes (1604-1875)*.
    Paris, 1904.
Weil, Peter M. "Political Structure and Process among the Gambia
    Mandinka: The Village Parapolitical System." In Carleton T.
    Hodge, ed., *Papers on the Manding*. Bloomington, Ind., 1971.
    Pp. 247-72.
White, Gavin. "Firearms in Africa: An Introduction." *JAH*,
    12:173-84 (1971).
Wilks, Ivor. "The Transmission of Islamic Learning in the
    Western Sudan." In Jack Goody, ed., *Literacy in Traditional
    Societies*. Cambridge, 1968. Pp. 162-97.
Wissett, Robert. *A Compendium of East India Affairs*. 2 vols.
    London, 1802.
Wood, W. Raymond. "An Archaeological Appraisal of Early European
    Settlements in the Senegambia. *JAH*, 8:39-64 (1967).
Wurie, A. "The Bundukas of Sierra Leone." *Sierra Leone Studies*,
    1 (new series):14-25 (1953).
Yule, H., and A. C. Burnell. *Hobson-Jobson*. London, 1903.
Zeltner, Frantz de. *Contes du Sénégal et du Niger*. Paris, 1913.
Zemp, Hugo. "La légende des griots malinké." *CEA*, 6:611-42
    (1966).
Zuccarelli, F. "Le régime des engagés à temps au Sénégal, 1817-
    48." *CEA*, 7:420-61 (1962).
Zupko, Ronald Edward. *A Dictionary of English Weights and
    Measures from Anglo-Saxon Times to the Nineteenth Century*.
    Madison, 1968.

INDEX

143

JACKET DESIGNED BY SYLVIA SOLOCHEK WALTERS

COMPOSED BY QUALITY TYPING SERVICE, MADISON, WISCONSIN

MANUFACTURED BY MALLOY LITHOGRAPHING, ANN ARBOR, MICHIGAN

Library of Congress Cataloging in Publication Data

Curtin, Philip D
Economic change in precolonial Africa.

Includes bibliographical references.
—— ——Supplementary evidence.
Bibliography: p.
1. Africa, West—Economic conditions. 2. Slave-
trade—Africa, West—History. 3. Africa, West—Com-
merce—History. I. Title.
HC503.W4C87Suppl   330.9'66'301   74-5899
ISBN 0-299-06640-1 (v. 1)
ISBN 0-299-06650-9 (suppl. v.)